*Revolutionary Cuba in the World Arena*_____

Revolutionary Cuba in the World Arena

edited by Martin Weinstein

A Publication of the
Institute for the Study of Human Issues
Philadelphia

Manufactured in the United States of America

Composition by Modern Typographers, Inc., Clearwater, Florida

Library of Congress Cataloging in Publication Data:

Main entry under title:

Revolutionary Cuba in the world arena.

    Includes bibliographies and index.
    1. Cuba—Foreign relations—1959–   Addresses, essays, lectures.
I. Weinstein, Martin. II. Institute for the Study of Human Issues.
F1788.R43   327.7291   79–10313
ISBN 0–915980–73–8

For information, write:

Director of Publications
ISHI
3401 Science Center
Philadelphia, Pennsylvania 19104
U.S.A.

For Kalman H. Silvert

Acknowledgments

The majority of the contributions to this volume derive from a conference on "The International Relations of the Cuban Revolution" sponsored by the Center for Latin American and Caribbean Studies of New York University in October–November 1975. The conference was generously supported by a grant from the Ford Foundation and was held in the gracious confines of the university's Maison Française. The Center's then director, Juan Corradi, was responsible for all organizational matters. He was ably assisted by Marcia Klugman and Alison McClure of the Center's staff.

Several additional chapters were commissioned after the conference, and extensive revisions have been made in the light of subsequent events. As editor, I would like to acknowledge the patience and professional care displayed by the contributors and the helpful suggestions from the editors at ISHI.

During the period of time between our meetings and the final production of this volume, Kalman Silvert, Professor of Politics at New York University, founding director of its Latin American Center, Program Advisor to the Ford Foundation, friend and colleague, passed away. It is fitting that this volume on the hemisphere's boldest experiment be dedicated, with love, to the man who gave so much to Latin American social science.

Martin Weinstein

Contents

Cuba's International Relations:
An Introduction

MARTIN WEINSTEIN

Revolution is rare, the building of a truly participant, egalitarian national community even rarer. Cuba has begun her Revolution. The forging of an integrated national community built on a literate, healthy, decently housed, reasonably well-fed, fully employed, socially useful, and meaningfully participant population has successfully begun. In some dimensions, it nears completion; in others, much remains to be done. But the infrastructure for socialism is there as are the possibilities for democracy. Whether Cuba gets its socialist democracy depends on the skills and attitudes of its leadership, the hard work of its people, the international climate, and the effective use made of that climate by the Cuban government.

It is this last aspect of the Cuban political process, its international relations, which is the subject of this volume. Obviously the other factors mentioned above cannot be kept separate from the subject at hand, but the contributors were asked to concentrate on factors affecting the international thrust of Cuba's political and economic life. Fortunately they have done so with a careful eye to the linkage of domestic and international politics.

The Revolution's nation-building successes give Cuba the ability to enter the world arena not merely as an object of invasion (the Bay of Pigs), as a pawn in a crisis between superpowers (the Missile Crisis), or simply as an exporter of guerrilla revolution, but rather as a model of a break with imperialism and, more importantly, of a road to development on which equity takes precedence over growth. In her essay for this volume, Frieda Silvert argues that Cuba's emergence as an

1

actor in the international arena requires the abandonment of the traditional dichotomies of "capitalist" and "socialist" if we are going to interpret meaningfully the Cuban Revolution and the promise and peril of its contemporary international relations.

Cuba is frequently described in the dependence literature as an example, perhaps the only one in Latin America, of a definitive and successful break with North American hegemony. The "dependence" paradigm explains the limits of economic development and the lack of social and political justice in the Third World as the result of domestic and international power configurations significantly determined by the international expansion of capitalism. In this context it is clear that as a socialist state formally committed to Marxism-Leninism and increasingly linked economically and politically to the Soviet bloc, Cuba has broken its dependence on the United States and with it, that "geographical fatalism" (as Nita Manitzas so aptly puts it in her chapter) which has colored hemispheric politics throughout this century.

Nevertheless, a closer examination of Cuba's economic performance indicates that previous conditions and available resources are variables which cannot be ignored or completely overcome even by as radical and dramatic a shift as Cuba has undergone since 1959. In this regard, the contributions to this volume by two economists, Gerald Hagelberg and Edward Hewett, are highly informative. In his thorough analysis of the sugar industry, Hagelberg reminds us that what was true for Cuba in 1958 is just as valid in 1978, namely that *sin azúcar, no hay país* (without sugar, there is no country). The ups and downs in production, the wide fluctuation in world prices, and, perhaps most importantly, the disruptions and misallocations caused by the attempt to produce a ten-million-ton harvest in 1970, have all had important effects on the course of the Revolution.

In addition, Cuba's heavy reliance on sugar exports to the Soviet Union and Eastern Europe, similar to her previous reliance on the U.S. market, highlights the continued political and economic implications of a one-crop economy. In spite of the favorable price Cuba receives for her exports to the Soviet bloc, such harsh realities as depressed world sugar prices, the removal of Cuba from the ranks of low-cost producers, and the fact that a significant increase in sugar prices (a situation not foreseen at this time) would once again stimulate the production of sugar substitutes like corn syrup, all harbinger a difficult road for a sugar-based economy.

It was the gamble with a ten-million-ton sugar harvest, and the failure of that venture, which turned Cuba increasingly toward a more standard, Eastern European planning and trade pattern. As Hewett argues in his essay, Cuba's formal entry in 1972 into the Council for

Mutual Economic Assistance (CMEA or COMECON) may have been generously kept at a low or negligible monetary cost by the Soviet Union, but there are other factors to be considered. The development of a Cuban five-year plan under CMEA coordination may actually complicate or impede integrated and autonomous economic development. Cuba could find herself a commodities supplier (sugar, nickel, and citrus fruits) to a much more industrialized Soviet bloc under trade arrangements and development plans that postpone or inhibit the industrialization of the island. Hewett concludes that Cuba's entry into CMEA is "a logical extension of Soviet pressure for system change in Cuba," which will move her in the direction of the centrally planned, bureaucratically organized societies of Eastern Europe. One result of increased integration with Eastern bloc economies is a restriction on Cuba's ability to diversify her trading partners which, in turn, may affect her desire or possibilities for significant resumption of trade with the United States should the normalization of relations continue to progress. I shall have more to say on this subject below.

As Hewett illustrates, the tactical stops and starts of Cuban foreign policy since 1959 are intimately related to domestic conditions and the success or failure of specific policies and goals. The early pyrotechnics of the Bay of Pigs and Missile Crisis gave way in ensuing years to a profound debate involving both domestic and foreign matters: the construction of socialism (e.g., moral versus material incentives), the nature of a socialist society (e.g., the creation of the "new man"), and an attempt to export revolution (guerrilla training, Che Guevara's role in Bolivia, etc.). But this period, from roughly 1962 to 1968, has been overanalyzed in terms of the surface changes of Cuban foreign policy, especially concerning Cuba's move from a pro-Soviet to a pro-Chinese outlook and then back to the Moscow perspective on world affairs. Such analysis has frequently overlooked the fundamental political task faced by Castro during that period: the preservation of the Cuban Revolution through the creation of new values and loyalties and the elimination of previous forms of economic and political dependence.

Cuba's principal strain with Moscow during these years reflected Fidel Castro's and Che Guevara's commitment to the export of revolution. Cuba's perception of the Kremlin's failure to support the revolutionary struggle in Latin America cooled relations. Fidel's qualified support for the invasion of Czechoslovakia and the death of Che in Bolivia indicated that Cuba's "maverick" era was coming to an end. But Fidel was prepared for one dramatic attempt to rekindle the spirit of revolution before he would definitively join the Soviet fold. The campaign for a ten-million-ton sugar harvest was the program chosen to mobilize the political and economic energies of the island. The failure of that harvest and the economic dislocations resulting from it translated into an increasing political and economic dependence on the Soviet Union.

However, despite these apparent changes in direction, and conceding the more orthodox path the Cuban Revolution has taken since the early 1970s, there has been an ideological consistency between Cuba's successful efforts at nation-building and its view of the role it should play in the international arena. As Nita Manitzas puts it in her essay:

> . . . Cuba's solidarity with the less developed tier of nations is an intrinsic element in the political socialization of every Cuban schoolchild. . . . It represents the projection onto the international stage of one of the fundamental strands of Cuba's internal, national ideology.

To underestimate the significance of the above observation is to seriously misinterpret Cuba's foreign policy, its meaning to the Cubans, and the independence or autonomy of their position. Whether disagreeing with Moscow over the export of violent revolution to the Latin American continent in the mid-1960s, or abandoning that effort by the early 1970s, Cuba has maintained a commitment to the struggles of the peoples of the Third World. Tactics may change, partly as a result of the changing international climate and partly as the result of domestic considerations of Soviet pressure, but the strategic goal of a weakening of "Western imperialism" has never been altered.

The Cuban Revolution has been consistently misinterpreted in— or ostracized from—the mainstream development literature, and that performance is not being improved upon in the endeavors by most social scientists and policymakers (frequently one and the same) to interpret and respond to recent Cuban moves on the international stage. Nowhere is this more obvious than in the efforts to explain, predict, or react to Cuban involvement in Africa and elsewhere in the Third World.

To see the Cubans as pawns or mercenaries for the Russians is to deny the history of Cuban solidarity and sacrifice in various areas of the world. It is true, as Professor Domínguez observes in his thoughtful chapter, that Cuban involvement in Angola and Ethiopia represents a significant departure from previous actions, in that it involves the commitment of regular Cuban armed forces in direct combat abroad. But this does not indicate that Moscow gave Havana its marching orders, even though Russia obviously approved of the activity and supplied the Cubans with their heavy arms and equipment.

Perhaps it is more plausible to see the commitment of regular Cuban troops in Africa as an expression of the security of the Cuban Revolution at home and the requirements, as judged by Havana, of effective solidarity with the black African left. No observer can ignore the pragmatism and opportunism involved in Cuba's high profile in Africa, but neither can one deny that Cuba has picked her allies and theaters of operation in Africa with a certain logic and justification even in terms of international law and diplomacy. Up to this time, her actions have not included the revolutionary intervention of Cuban guerrillas against an established government. This would change if the situation in southern Africa deteriorated and the Cubans offered direct support to the black majority in a civil war against the Rhodesian or South African government.

Obviously Cuba is playing high-risk international power politics in Africa. The costs at home, as Domínguez indicates in this volume, have been an increased militarization of the society and the allocation of important human resources, including engineers, technicians, and medical personnel, outside the country. International costs may involve a lessening of Cuba's status as a nonaligned Third World nation. How significant that designation is to Cuba is not clear. Nevertheless, Havana has been framing her struggle for recognition and leadership in the Third World as primarily a North-South (the developed world versus the less developed world) and not an East-West (socialist versus capitalist) problematic. The African situation has pushed Western and especially some high-level U.S. perception of Cuba into the old ideological mold of an East-West (read "Cold War") problematic. Rightly or wrongly Cuba thus risks the possibility of seeing its relationship with the United States thrown back to the global politics of a Missile Crisis or the even more ideologically determined Bay of Pigs invasion. Perhaps Havana feels that such potential calamities are not likely under a Carter administration. But the increasingly conservative mood of domestic American politics, and the concern over human rights violations committed by the Soviet Union in the treatment of its dissidents, make the African situation a touchy one, potentially explosive for East-West relations. Cuba's involvement in Africa increases the probability that a renewal of the Cold War will have a high cost for Cuba.

It is conceivable, of course, that Cuba's leaders, having analyzed the risks involved, decided that the most immediate and perhaps the only direct international cost would be a halt or even regression on the path to normalization of U.S.-Cuban relations. In his hypothetical memorandum written for this volume, Abraham Lowenthal has captured the debate and calculations that most likely concerned the Cuban elite as they decided upon involvement in Angola. Fidel Castro no doubt considered the fact that his African policy would slow the momentum toward rapprochement that was expected to develop under the Carter administration in Washington, but when some of the variables are considered the costs of a delay are not very high. In the first place, the potential for significant trade with the U.S. has been reduced by Cuba's increased integration into the Soviet trade bloc. As for the hostility of the Cuban exile community, as Lourdes Casal accurately observes in her contribution, most Cubans in the U.S. are reconciled to the existence of a communist Cuba, and although the tension over Africa fuels the violent anti-Castro fringe that still exists, neither they nor the more passive majority have ever been more than marginal ingredients and/or expedient tools of United States policy toward Havana. As for the American public in general, the strong public sentiment against the successfully completed Panama Canal treaties surely indicates to Castro that U.S. public opinion, still heavily influenced by Cold War ideology, would oppose rapid and complete normalization of relations with Cuba even under the best of circumstances.

In sum, the survival of the Cuban Revolution does not seem to be threatened by Cuba's actions, thus far, in Africa. However, if Cuba is identified with Russian expansion in Africa and U.S.-Soviet détente collapses, Cuba runs the risk of becoming a victim of renewed East-West conflict. This outcome, however, might occur even without the presence of a single Cuban soldier in Africa. Most likely, Castro and his advisers are prepared to believe that Cuban-U.S. relations will continue to improve slowly; are convinced their Revolution will survive; and view the health, educational, and other benefits enjoyed by the masses of Cuba as a lesson not lost on their Caribbean neighbors and other Third World countries. The Cuban leadership probably believes that an international policy grounded in solidarity with and sacrifice for peoples of the Third World and based on the judicious use of Cuba's resources and military power can only enhance Cuba's stature and demonstrate the efficacy of her path. The stakes are high, but Cuban politics has been among the riskiest in the world for the last twenty years. The costs of this politics have been ample, including the delay in integrated economic growth with its concomitant denial of domestic consumer satisfaction and an ominous postponement of political and intellectual pluralism; but the gains are no less real or impressive, not the least of which has been the influence (real or imagined) that Cuba and her Revolution continue to exert in the world arena.

The Cuban Problematic

FRIEDA M. SILVERT

> Don't overlook the realities. In competition with the world's
> strongest nation, the leader [Fidel Castro] of a weak island
> country has outwitted the United States, broken out of isola-
> tion to renew diplomatic ties with almost the entire world
> and has helped win two wars in Africa. / A "knowledgeable
> analyst," *Newsweek,* 1978[1]
>
> Cuba is a small country, but it has a big country's foreign
> policy. / Jorge Domínguez, *Foreign Affairs,* 1978[2]

The Western world has not yet been able to come to terms with the
fundamental difference between Cuba's socialist development and all
other such experiments. Neither has the socialist world. To wit: The
Cuban experiment is the first successful socialism conceived and ex-
ecuted by its own citizens which has taken place in a fully Westernized
society.* Its culture is rooted in the democratic ethos of the Enlightenment. It is a society which, despite (or because of) the domination of
the Spanish and North Americans, has been fully aware, through a
century of struggle for independence, of the revolutionary dream for
democratic liberation set forth by the French Revolution. It is to this
dream that young Castro spoke—wittingly or not—when he said "history will absolve us." Thus, it is to the Enlightenment's dictum that
"man can be free" that we must turn if we are to understand modern
Cuba at home and abroad.

In answer to the possibility of freedom, two politics were developed in Western culture—the politics of capitalism and the politics
of socialism. Both address themselves to the historical realities of the

*This includes Cuba's black and Carib population.

coexistence of the conditions for equality and inequality within and among societies. Both promise equality, but not the quality of freedom as liberation. They differ on how, where, and when. The practical politicking of both is to defer the promise, justifying the present either by talk of the necessity for differential monetary and/or power rewards due to a hierarchy in societal developmental needs or by calling on the historical necessity of the "dictatorship of the proletariat" to correct past inequities. In the politics of capitalism, politics and the economy are made to appear as separate sub-autonomous realms despite Adam Smith's argument to the contrary. In the politics of socialism, politics and the economy are explicitly united in the concept of political economy according to Karl Marx.

In 1959 Cuba entered the politics of socialism. Her progress since then, however, cannot be understood without reference to the dialectics of transformation which in the relative short run are reflected in a *politic of transition*. For Cuba, this means that she is not free from the specifics of her social and cultural history, especially the legacy of dependency. Cuba must rid herself of old inequalities (class) at the same time that she is becoming subject in her everyday planning to new types of inequalities from within (techno-bureaucratic elites) and domination from one or the other adversary in the old and wearisome politics of the Cold War. This politic of transition does not only reflect a change in developmental direction; rather, it is a politic which explicitly searches for a unity between personal liberation and social innovation and thus touches base in Western societies with the eighteenth-century dream of a fully democratic society. It is not merely a politic of change in social organization; it is the politics of an historical movement which has as its mission the termination of all forms of domination. It is part of a social movement found in all modern societies whatever their cultural base. That is fundamentally why Cuba is important.

In the playing out of the responses to the new dialectic, certain attitudinal modalities seem to be emerging on the international scene, creating a new set of rules of the game for both the politician and the student of politics. One of the emerging modalities raises to greater prominence the emancipatory capacities of people; it is based on the processual nature of social reality, the fact that historical alternatives exist within a cultural matrix as viable visions and are made possible by people's choices to act.[3] The other modality negates this possibility, promising a technology of social justice without freedom of choice. But, for both modalities in the new politics, the old questions "for whom" and "for what" take on greater salience than they do in the old modalities of capitalism and communism, while politics is given a greater weight in the attempt to reintroduce the precepts of political economy into the affairs among nations. The new politics—and the dialectics in which Cuba finds herself immersed—go beyond capitalism and communism. *The new politics is engaged with another order of difference: that between authoritarianism and liberation.*

That is why Cuba's reorganization is an "experiment." That is why Cuban actions in the health field, in education, in Angola, in Ethiopia, in Bolivia, in seeking détente with the United States, and in her role in the Third World should not be viewed simply as probes by a new partner in the "old politics" of capitalism and communism. Cuba is in the forefront of something different. Otherwise, surely, we have witnessed a miracle. Imagine how many more small and not-so-small countries would now have hope that they too might have a big country's global influence given the right constellation of aid by star performers.

It is my proposition that the Cuban experiment will develop in relation to the new dialectics and the forces of transformation they engender. I do not believe it possible to understand Cuban actions (or the reactions to them) in the old terms of balance of power, encirclement, containment, Cold War, Pan-Africanism, socialist hegemony, oil, sugar, or stages of development. For, if we try, policymakers will always be beset with surprises, dilemmas, or crises (as they have been for so many decades), and students of politics must continue to twist their readings of "the situation" with long lists of on-the-one-hands and on-the-other-hands, or even resort to the infamous "great man" syndrome. Examples of perplexities caused by the old categories are numerous. To mention but the most recent: how do we comprehend, as Andrew Young, the U.S. Ambassador to the United Nations, pointed out,[4] the fact that Angolans are protecting American interests with Cuban troops and supplying Americans with almost a billion dollars' worth of oil a year despite the United States' active opposition to the MPLA; or that Cuba has played a moderating role in Ethiopia and Eritrea as had the United States two years previously;[5] or, more embarrassing, that President Carter had to temper his first reactions to the supposed Cuban connection with the Zaire affair, after his initial burst of Cold War rhetoric, while he continued to condone French and Belgian interference? And how do we treat a much more troubling "dilemma"—Cuba's apparent ability to solve unsolvable internal developmental problems and increase participatory involvement by all Cubans, but its simultaneous inability to dispose of the ancient myth that there must be "leaders" and "followers" for the good of the "larger" society (democratic-centralism).

It is not enough to say that Cuba follows a different drummer sometimes—and sometimes not.[6] What seems to be more important is to capture the beat, however self-contradictory it may appear to be.

Nor is it enough to say that Cuba's official ideology is not of the biblical variety (Moscow's line). What seems more important is whether Cuba will be a force in the "new politics," successfully fulfilling her claims to uniqueness by creating independence and equality in her own society as well as assisting other countries to do the same; or whether she will be a "cat's paw" in the "old politics." The progress of her experiment is the source of the Cuban problematic. Will the Cubans opt only for social justice or will they choose social liberation? Will Cuba help solve the calculus of equality and inequality so that freedom is a real quality of everyday life?

Washington and Havana

> In politics as in religion, the facts can be misleading. What matters most is belief, emotional response, interpretation, desire, hope, faith. The historic causes of the Revolution are what the Cubans of Castro's generation believe them to be. Any other interpretation is quarreling with *Cuban* history. How Cubans ought to think and feel is an academic exercise; how Anglo-Saxon observers feel about the Revolution is largely beside the point. / Herbert Matthews, former editor, *New York Times,* 1975[7]

It is not the first time that we have had to wait for the exquisite and economical insight of a journalist to make clear a seemingly perplexing dilemma. The pity is we must wait so long. The United States and Cuba have, of course, been caught in a clumsy and sometimes inglorious *pas de deux* of irreverent and irrelevant misunderstandings since 1959. And, of course, the cause of this has been their different evaluations of what "ought to be" in their own best interests and what in fact "is becoming." The turns in the dynamic of making history have muted the beginnings of the controversy, permitting the more reasonable everyday compromise. Hard-core assessments as well as policymakers' reevaluations, however, still seem to slip into the realm of the gut or become entangled in one or another ideology.

Finding agreeable conditions of détente between Washington and Havana is more complex in the late seventies than it was in 1959. For the United States, the obvious complexity is that settling the "Cuban Question" is no longer a comfortable unilateral matter. The more serious difficulty, however, is how to thread one's way through the Cuban experiment's ties to the Third World phenomenon, to the growing demand for a more equitable distribution of the world's goods between industrialized and nonindustrialized countries, and to the tactics used by the raw-material producing nations of subjecting their economic needs to political goals (the reintroduction of political economy in foreign affairs). The visible non-national politicking of global corporations only makes the internationalized equality debate more complex and conditions of détente more intricate; it does not mute the issue. Neither does Cuba's African incursion. Rather, the staying power of the Cuban Revolution—whose proclaimed ends are to change its dependent status and create internal equality—and the demonstrated ability of the Cuban leadership to carry out a "global" foreign strategy make it all the more clear that the break in Cuba's isolation since 1975 is not only a local hemispheric affair but one which has international ramifications.

The first visible thaw in Cuban/U.S. relations began more or less in 1974, and since then relations have alternated between the sour and not-so-sour. In the fall of 1976, the Cuban question in the United States was plucked from the dark provinces of the anti-Cuban lobbyists and placed in the political marketplace of debatable domestic issues. The new Carter administration, wanting to change the North American image in Latin American capitals, indicated along with its more concentrated efforts to finalize a new Panama Canal treaty (ratified by the U.S. Senate in early 1978) that it was ready to sweeten the Cuban relationship.[8] The Linowitz Commission, an ad hoc committee of private citizens, advised the new president of certain public opinions on two separate occasions. Among its other recommendations it called for the resumption of talks with Cuba as well as the finalization of a new Panama Canal treaty. Newspapers and television networks have done new documentaries on modern Cuba since 1975 and, in correspondence with Washington's diplomatic reading of the thaw's progress, have presented to the American polity their findings on the new Cuba. Businessmen are visiting and talking with Cuban officials about renewing trade agreements. Many Latin American countries have put aside OAS sanctions against Cuba and reestablished diplomatic missions in Havana. Cuba's cooperation with the Angolan MPLA soured the process. Nevertheless, American tourists are once again going to Havana, this time not to visit with Lady Luck at the gambling tables but to see what Lady Luck has bestowed on a bigger gamble, the Cuban people's attempt to roll the dice for a better society.

President Carter's implementation of the Trilateral Commission's recommendation that the West develop a collective global strategy is bearing fruit: Washington is paying less attention to its old special-relation policy towards Latin America and now negotiates with each country on a case-by-case basis as it affects global policies. And President Carter's emphasis on human rights has had dramatic echoes in Latin America, despite the unevenness of its application and its lower priority in Washington's list of global problems.

These moves have not brought about an abrupt change in hemispheric relations with the Cubans, but they have changed the tone of discourse in the United States: the "never, unless . . ." Cuban Question has become more of the "maybe, because, if . . ." Cuban Issue. Knowing what the Cubans are all about is no longer the flexing of mere academic muscle or ideological intransigence; it is now an ingredient of practical politics for Americans.

The Nature of Cuban Development*

The social and political feel in Cuba is one of relaxation. One can engage in political debate, even in direct disagreement with Cubans, and incur no open hostility. Hints of impatience of course surface, but that is the fare of all first steps in political thaws. These hints are helpful, however, for they reveal more fully what Cubans perceive their task to be, how engrossed and dedicated they are to it, and what their myopias might be.

Cubans, for example, will tell you that criticism is welcome, but only within the frame of a general sympathy with the goals of Cuba's Revolution. Their request is legitimate and understandable. Why should Cubans have to defend themselves against attitudes that question the fundamentals of their national being and ideological premises? But, even within the ground rules of positive empathy, the request is most difficult to honor at first blush. The reason is that the very determination of the frame of reference within which Cuba fits is a troublesome problem. To unravel the Cuban problematic in both its surface aspect of "dilemma" as well as its position within the larger social movement of which Cuba claims to be a part, it is important to examine the nature of the victory Cuba has won and is now beginning to enjoy. Is it truly a socialist victory or one of another kind? For, let

---

*This section is taken, in large part, from an article entitled "Fate, Chance, and Faith" written by Kalman H. and Frieda M. Silvert after a visit to Cuba in July 1974. The article was published originally as an American Universities Field Staff Report, North America Series, Vol. 2, No. 2 (September 1974) and was reprinted in Kalman H. Silvert, *Essays in Understanding Latin America* (Philadelphia: Institute for the Study of Human Issues, 1977).

there be no doubt—the Cubans have won something. That is why the air of relaxation. The aroma of embattlement is gone in Cuba and Cubans take pride in their progress.

Nonetheless, Cubans are troubled by the ideological racket made by those who do not understand their historical uniqueness and become impatient with those who do not feel that Cubans are doing the very best they can to work out their own destiny. C. Wright Mills, in his early book on Cuba, *Listen, Yankee!*, reported correctly that Cuba's revolutionary leaders were adamantly convinced that they had not been scarred by the Marxist ideological wars of the 1930s and 1940s. But no European or North American political person, whether of leftist or rightist persuasion, can cross out of his or her mind Stalinism, Central European totalitarianism, Tito and the national question in socialist development, or even the widespread student disorders of the 1960s and their evanescent and shifting ideological components. In truth, the Cubans have not been immune, either. As Cuba's revolution has taken form, the radical "liberationism" of Guevara has been shelved (momentarily, most Cubans will tell you) and Cuba's "new man" bears many marks of the old one. Some material incentives are back, and attempts are being made to get away from artificial pricing and into some mechanism that will permit demand to affect supply through an ordered market. Premier (now President) Castro and the Cuban Communist Party have openly declared their adherence to the organizational form of democratic-centralism, a structural type of government propounded by Lenin in answer to Russia's underdevelopment in 1917 after the November Revolution.

Withal, the Cuban leadership does have its own vision, one heavily influenced by Cuban history (Cubans have been in a war of independence since their thirty-year war against Spain, 1868–98) and the obvious fact that Cuba is a part of the Americas. As a result, Cuban culture is infused with a set of attitudes about functional democracy, the role of persons in society, and personal freedom which lean more to the idiosyncratic democratic ethos of North America (and in some ways to nineteenth-century Spanish liberal thought) than to the democratic-centralism of the Soviets. The truth of this lies not only in the Cuban leadership's claim to uniqueness, but in the flavor of the island, in how Cubans work, sweat, and enjoy their Revolution and now, in one way or another, they bring an irrepressible Cuban flair into their everyday lives. Mardi Gras is still an extravaganza, no longer symbolic of the beginning of Lent, yet not dimmed by its economic usefulness in siphoning off excess currency which would otherwise feed the black market. Cuban women still frequent beauty shops, despite the grimness of revolutionary tasks; they paint their nails, set their hair, and otherwise indulge in "bourgeois" habits. Although they are very much concerned with the specifics of women's liberation—which they have yet to achieve—they remain, above all else, Cubans seeking the Cuban way. And then there is the infamous Tropicana night club, alive and well in Havana, creating a new art form out of a debased one as it nightly helps to celebrate the Revolution.

> *Moral One of the Problematic:* Cubans share with North Americans, as they do with other Latin Americans, the history of Western culture, and in particular, that part of the democratic ethos which enables ordinary citizens to say "no" to oppression and domination.

CUBA'S INTERNAL TAPESTRY OF TRANSFORMATION

Cuba has either already solved or is well on the way to solving every standard problem whose solution development specialists seek in their work, be they socialist, capitalist, or Third World enthusiasts.

Population.   There is no population explosion in Cuba. As of 1970 the official birth rate was 1.91, down from the annual rate of increase of 3.31 in the early 1900s. Present practice is to wrap family planning into general health care.

Health.   Cuba's health coverage has been widely and favorably observed. It is said to be a truly national system. At present life expectancy for men is 71 years and for women almost 74 years. Comparable figures for Argentina are 67.1 for both sexes, for Ecuador 52.3, and for the United States 70.8 (1970). More important from a social standpoint, health care has been taken out of the money economy: it has become an inalienable right for all.

Employment.   Cuba has only fractional unemployment. Even though the population is young (a third of all Cubans have been born since 1959), 47.3 percent are economically active. The unemployment rate in 1970 was 1.3 percent, as contrasted with 8.4 percent in 1953, the year Fulgencio Batista was installed as president by a military coup.

Unemployment, underemployment, and sporadic employment were endemic problems in Cuba in the past, given the nature of seasonal work in the fields. There is now a labor shortage in Cuba. But, as is often pointed out by foreign critics as well as in the public speeches of Cuban officials, inexpertness and low productivity were a major problem until recently. Leaving aside the varying quality of work, a comparative occupation profile between 1953 and 1970 (see Table 1) shows the change toward employment patterns typical of more fully developed countries.

*Table 1 | Shifts in the Economically Active Population
(over 10 Years of Age) in Cuba, 1953–1970*

Economic Sector	1953	1970
Farming	41.5%	30.1%
Industry	17.4	20.0
Construction	3.3	5.7
Transportation and communications	4.9	6.4
Commerce[a]	20.3	12.0
Services	11.0	23.1
Others	1.6	2.7

[a]The drop in the figure for commerce is the only atypical change.
It reflects Cuba's state collectivism, of course.

Education.　Like health care, the Cuban educational system has
been widely hailed abroad. The first great push was for literacy. The
illiteracy rate now could scarcely be lowered. The second great push
was in primary education. Since 1958–59, the number of schools as well
as enrollment has been doubled, the great expansion taking place in
the countryside—from 4,889 schools to 12,731 (1971–72). The third big
effort is now being made in the secondary schools, the level of education which, in Latin America, has traditionally separated lower- from
middle-class students. The announced desire of the Cuban government
is to do away with the idea of an educational pyramid—that is, to turn
Cuba into a modern evocation of the old French rationalists' dream
of an *estado docente*, a teaching society in which education proceeds at
all levels, ages, and walks of life. This ideal is mixed with the Marxist
vision of creating a truly universal man, one who is equally at home
in intellectual pursuits, farm work, industry, and in the fruitful pursuit
of leisure.

The marriage of these two ideas, made into a triangle by the labor
shortage, results in the work-study plans that characterize all education
from primary school up. For example, most of the new secondary
schools are *secundarios en el campo*, "schools in the country." Students
reside at the school and are responsible for their academic curriculum
as well as three hours' work a day in the fields. Truck farming and the
production of citrus and other specialized export crops are already
making important use of this student labor. At the university level, all
students are expected to spend twenty hours a week in paid work. The
first year is usually dedicated to unskilled tasks, after which the work

duties are increasingly related to the career being followed by the student.

The universities, except for their faculties of engineering, medicine, and related skills as well as the recent addition of law, have received less attention. Questions of academic freedom, university autonomy, and the role of the intellectual in Cuban society remain thorny, tied as they invariably are to the ideological racket that makes Cubans impatient.

Food and Agriculture. Rural affairs have been subject to the most intense ideological debate and confusion of any aspect of Cuban governmental activity since 1959. Dependence on sugar, attempts to diversify, food shortages, the vagaries of the international market, and the ruralist romanticism of the revolution's leaders have played themselves out around questions of how to organize the national economy and, within it, the role of country people. In this process, the star of Ernesto "Che" Guevara rose and fell. Whatever the past, even in this sphere a turning point has been reached. The watershed was the sugar harvesting failure of 1970, a failure in which some say the greatest Cuban success was born. The failure helped cause the Cubans to readjust their economic goals with even greater national dedication to the aims of the Revolution.

The world price of sugar remains a problem, but Cuba still has a buffer in her trade with the Soviets, who buy Cuban sugar at prices higher than the price set in the U.S. Water storage facilities are being increased dramatically throughout the island, promising stability in the cultivation of such diverse crops as rice and cotton. The citrus crop is beginning to be profitable in the export market. Truck farming is improving, and vegetables and fruits are not in such short supply as even a few years ago. Fish and seafood were plentiful as of 1974; beef, chicken, and pork were not. Milk and dairy products, major sources of protein, have become commonplace staples. In short, there is enough to eat for everyone, although much remains to be done on the foreign-exchange scene and national food tastes have yet to be satisfied.

Urbanization. It may wryly be said that pollution is no problem in Cuban cities. There are very few cars. This is changing, however, as a result of recent trade agreements with American-owned subsidiaries in Latin America. There is little problem with crowding, even though the urban population of the island rose from 51 percent in 1953 to about 60 percent in 1975. Despite the decrease in rural occupations and the increase in typically urban service and industrial undertakings, the population flow to the cities has been absorbed by new towns located in the countryside and by the construction of large, integrated town-like housing developments in areas surrounding the three major cities.

As in the matter of higher education, however, the subtlety of the problem is not suggested by numbers. Havana has visibly been neglected, for example. Informal governmental estimates (1974) have it that merely putting Havana back into its prerevolutionary physical condition (a project now on the drawing boards of Cuban planners) will cost some three hundred million U.S. dollars. For the usual town planner, Cuba's urban problems are not great. For the social thinker, though, they are massive.

Havana is something of a shock, not because it is not painted, but because there is little milling on the streets and sidewalks, except around hotels and communications centers. The random clabbering expected of so large a metropolis does not occur; there is no whey in which social curds can form, to be rejected or made part of the cultural ethos. A demographic concentration, even well provided with clean water, sewage systems, and roofs, does not a city make. But what, after all, is any city to do if it is stripped of its commerce? (North Americans need only look at the wastelands of suburbia.) Take away the shopping areas, the eating places, and the sense of variety which the exchange of goods and ideas (capitalist or socialist) brings with it and "city style" must suffer, as must the ebb and flow of individual movement. The "city" is reduced to its classical pre-urbane functions: a place to work, an administration center, a transportation hub, a place to sleep, a place to get away from. (For the people of Havana, getting away means going to spectacular Lenin Park and the not-too-distant beaches.)

The Cubans have a particular difficulty in thinking about the city. Almost all the revolutionary leaders were born outside Havana, and came to the capital for their higher education. Despite the fact that their success was made possible by city people both in Cuba and abroad, they have practiced a revolution based on the rapid underwriting of social change in rural areas and small towns. This process has a fundamental justification: it is a major step on the way to reducing urban-rural differences, to carrying communications and services equally to all parts of the relatively small and manageable land that is Cuba. Thus, the relative *physical* neglect of Havana has been balanced by the educational, health, and organizational integration of all the other Cubans into participant local communities.

Not only Cubans, but apparently all socialists have trouble thinking about cities. Although they find it easy to see the falseness in the current dichotomy between town and country in capitalist societies, their solutions are tinged with an idyllic utopian ruralism. At issue is not only whether there is a functional substitute for the play of competition in economic, artistic, or ideational pursuits (i.e., whether competition can be divested of the egotistic and profit motive), but also what the long-term consequences may be of the almost overbearing emphasis placed by ongoing experiments in socialism on purely economic tasks. Perhaps it is because such experiments have been successfully started only in developing countries, as in the Cuban case, that much attention has perforce been given to discipline in work and economic interaction. But, at this moment, one cannot avoid the conclusion that in the politics of socialism an anti-intellectualism and rural traditional populism combine with the city's historical role as the seat of bourgeois values to create a socialist anti-urban bias equaled in intensity only by the city-hatred of green-belt romantics in Western democracies. Whether it be in New York, Paris, Havana, or Peking, to plan only for order and increasing rationalization is to invite mere technical responses to a situation that touches on the core of cultural style and personal liberation. Cuban urban planners seem much like their counterparts in the United States. Their worries are quite literally only concrete.

Participation. The achievements of the Cuban government noted above are relatively easy to measure. Much more difficult is the matter of participation. Almost everyone in Cuba takes participation to be a good in itself. So organizations are legion, and organization is universal. There are the civil defense organization (the *cederistas* or CDRists), women's organizations, trade unions, the Communist Party, block and neighborhood associations, and all other manner of cells, collectives, and institutions. Added to these are the beginnings of elective participation—the first instance of which took place in 1974 in the province of Matanzas, not too far from the capital. The basic reason for continuing voluntary labor in the fields is to further this organized mixing of the population. The subject need not be belabored. The point is that organization is complex, based on cement sidewalks as well as grass roots, and open to all. At this level, participation is real and effective: justice is dispensed at the bottom for minor crimes and misdemeanors; university curricula are developed through meetings involving all those affected by the academic offerings; even the slowly evolving legal codes are checked with organized groups in neighborhoods and provincial villages.

Whether this universality of belonging and publicly doing is "good" or "bad" is not the question at this moment; it exists, and serves to complete this summary of the dream of the routine developmentalist. In the material aspects of life, and in the basic social organization of the local community, Cuba has met the prescriptions of the hortatory statements about development one finds in the reports of the World Bank, the Inter-American Development Bank, the Agency for International Development, the Agricultural Development Council, and all the rest of our grand gamut of assistance agencies. It has also more than met the prescriptions of the Soviets' various five- and ten-year plans, Yugoslavia's modernization drive in its southern sector, the Chinese drive for total mobilization of town and country, and all the other smaller socialist plans to foster development and create equality among people. Cuba has done all of these things in a relatively short time, albeit in a small and manageable area. But,

—The *quantitative* facts of development do not assure the *qualitative* essence of a good social life.

—Egalitarianism is not *equity*.

—Increasing the number of urban persons does not increase the number of *urbane* ones.

—Increasing the number of rural persons does not increase the number of *liberated* ones.

—The *indicators* of development are not development.

—Participation is not *democracy*.

> *Moral Two of the Problematic*: The successes of the Cuban Revolution prove, if not beyond a shadow of a doubt, certainly within reasonable limits, that the eco-technical solutions to developmental problems are simple, if the *political* choice is made to give them first priority.

> *Corollary*: The near-total involvement of the Cuban people in developmental tasks does not "prove" that *participation* necessarily breeds either liberation or authoritarianism. However, it does suggest that participation may be better understood in the short run as *mobilization* for certain prescribed goals.

PATTERNS IN THE CUBAN EXPERIMENT

Pluses. Although the consequences of Cuba's technical success are not yet fully played out, they stand as an alternative pattern, especially for the Third World, to the favored mechanistic "trickle-down" theory of economic developmentalists such as Milton Friedman in the West and the macro-planners of socialist countries. Even though Cuba's experiment may not be directly applicable to the specific historical conditions of other countries, its demonstration effect poses a set of crucial questions: Must countries, once committed to fuller development, be continually plagued by the possible backlash of built-up delayed gratification (violence in the streets and fields)? Must the governors continually be justifying the growing absolute distance in real income between the social classes (i.e., poverty) by offering the carrot of equality in the future? Must developing societies continually engage in momentary but absolute violent practices against human and civil rights (totalitarianism)? And, finally, must the promised liberation from anti-human labor be stymied by the apparently increasing inability of technical elites to do more than solve short-run problems (disdevelopment by incompetence)? And, if the raising of these questions creates discomfort for the singleminded, the Cuban revolutionary experiment adds yet another more spectacular political accomplishment: it has forged the first truly national community in Latin America. It has been able, as a complement to its material gains, to institute a nation-state, one that is secular, partially egalitarian, aiming toward total participation, able to call on its people to show ultimate loyalty to fellow Cubans despite new status-derived differences. With this unequivocal victory, Cuba has joined the modern world—an accomplishment that evokes admiration, but not without worry. For the creation of national community, as has been historically demonstrated, may be the precondition for socially despicable or for admirable societies; for a more total authoritarianism or a more fully liberated democracy.

The political significance of Cuba's double-barrelled demonstration is not lost on the new nations that are caught in the Catch-22 syndrome of balancing internal immediate needs with external uncontrollable realities. Neither is it lost on the United States and the rest of the so-called developed world. After all, it is these successes which have made it possible for us, as well as others, to begin again to talk with Cuba on national co-equal terms and for the Cubans to take affirmative action in international politics.

> *Moral Three of the Problematic*: The formation of a political structure of total national community is a precondition for modernizing development.
>
> *Corollary*: In the United States and the rest of the industrialized world, Cuba's accomplishment informs policymakers that the historic "special relationship" of the United States with Cuba, and most probably with the rest of Latin America, had come to an end even before Washington adopted its "global" strategy.

Minuses.   As Cuba emerges from isolation, it has much of the quantitative wherewithal to face the more complex task of defining for itself the quality of life it wants—what Carlos Rafael Rodríguez calls "building socialism" and others call "institutionalizing the revolution."

However phrased, there is a recognition among Cubans that they have as yet to make the Socialist Revolution, a job which involves, at a minimum, connecting the present patterns of local participation with effective national participation—the passage to governance instead of government—and, in the longer run, the creation of full freedom, which demands the growth of new needs coupled with the permissiveness and ability of society to fulfill them.

Most Cubans in high positions know this to be the imminent task. They are, also, a worried leadership without help from compatible cultural and ideational models, and burdened by consequences of decisions made during their isolated, survival years. They are well aware that they have not completely altered their dependent status—in large measure, they believe, because of the American embargo, which has led them to seek assistance and trade almost wherever it was offered. (Besides Soviet aid, for example, they accepted refrigerator ships from Franco's Spain.)

Although the Cuban citizen is organized at many different levels, as has been pointed out earlier, and is even beginning to have an elective choice between opposing views in local affairs, he or she has no say in national planning or foreign affairs. The Cuban leadership still counts on—and gets—consensus by loyalty to the Revolution and to Fidel Castro. Ideological differences are still considered unrevolutionary, and intellectuality in the form of critical reflection on one's condition is not yet an acceptable proposition in Cuba. Emphasis is on the *work ethic and productivity,* which seem to have become almost a creed among Marxist-Leninists who have led successful revolutions in developing countries. (These aspects of the Protestant Ethic apparently fit well with developmental needs, be they socialist or capitalist.) And, although there is concern about the lack of creativity among middle managers and technicians, Cubans continue to stress technical skills.

In Cuba the newspaper *Granma* and other house organs remain closed and parochial. They serve party functions and they may educate, but they do not give news. Radio and television are the same. Unfortunately, only a few Cubans are disturbed by this. Movie-making is better, as is poster art. Leisure space and architecture are sometimes breathtaking and humane, but living arrangements remain underdeveloped. The planners' conception of the "house," which almost always means a multi-dwelling, is that of a functionalism based on their Marxist misconception of urbanity and their traditional adherence to "bourgeois" limits imposed by the use of space for profit. Cubans are not too troubled about this aspect; they feel they have first to provide minimum housing, and later the question of real living space may be put on the drawing boards. Status-position still makes a difference in determining who goes to the more advanced secondary schools and the university. (In 1974, for instance, it was estimated that 40 percent of the children who went to Cuba's famous Lenin School came from the white-collar functionary elite.) Cubans, however, are very worried about this continuing inequity and there has already been a push to change the ratio.

To be sure, this accounting of the negative aspects of the Cuban experiment's progress to date is not complete. Neither was our affirmative one. They are meant to highlight the dialectics of transformation as they have been played out in Cuba since 1959. The point is that there are contradictory movements, historical and systemic, to which Cubans must find answers. One small example in the important area of law may help illustrate the difficult interplay between revolutionary and practical needs. Many of the revolutionary leaders, including President Castro, were trained as lawyers but despised the uses to which the law was put; therefore, the university reform of 1962 reflected a desire to improve technical training and to downgrade the law. Legal studies became so despised that in 1969 only 11 students were enrolled in the law school of the University of Havana, the only one in the country. As someone in the faculty of law was said to have remarked, Cuba was getting to the stage "of being all revolution and no law." In the early years of the Revolution the notion was that the revolutionary spirit would provide justice, but this proved to be not enough. It was not until 1969, after seven years of experience with Popular Tribunals (which still exist) and after the first steps to institutionalize the revolution had been taken, that a new legal code began to be formulated. It was the dean of the law faculty who explained the dynamic involved: it was just because Cuba was not yet a socialist society that law was a continuing necessity and therefore had to be reconstituted.

In sum, the Cuban experiment cannot be denied its phenomenal gains. The future of Cuban socialism hangs on how the country will handle the translation of its developmental successes into the quality of its vision. Its progress to date falsifies all so-called theories of development, all the politicians' excuses, and puts to shame all those who would deny a people's capacity to fight for conditions that make it possible for them to control their own destiny. The Cuban experiment is not ossified. It continues to cope with the legacy of colonialism and the necessity for rapid economic development by seeking diversified trade and technological transfers, which never come free of ideological baggage. The Cuban experiment is still innovative. Cubans have demonstrated their ability to develop a unity between the economy and politics and thus have gained greater flexibility. They have placed politics above economics despite pressing material need; they built national community before socialism;* they decided to integrate the countryside into the nation instead of focusing on the urban economic asset which was already in place; they decided to allow the professional and middle class to leave the country, thereby losing precious technical and administrative resources; and they have decided to come to the aid of authentic liberation movements, thereby endangering the very existence of the experiment's life.

Cuba still searches for a method to satisfy her vision of a socialist world. The Cuban leadership's latest choice to act in African conflicts should be seen as connected to this search. Perhaps some believe that the choice has not always been on target, or that the choice should never have been entertained in the first place, or worse, that it may turn out to be counterproductive to the experiment itself. But to exercise choice either by commission or omission ensures neither success nor truth. What matters is that the Cubans are engaged in a transformation. Although Cuba has done much in isolation, continued transformation and growth have demanded of the small island its emergence into the larger arena of world economics, politics, and technological transfers. Having built the foundations of a social nation, it was ready. Even without recognition by the United States—it would have been infinitely less traumatic with it—Cuba has taken its place among nations.

The Cuban Revolution and International Affairs

> It is time that one overcomes the ridiculous myth of the invincible Cubans. Who ever heard of Cubans conducting a global foreign policy? We must make clear to other countries that we will not be blackmailed by Cuban troops. . . .
> / Henry Kissinger, 1978[9]

> It [the Cuban presence in Angola] has created a kind of psychological impotence among some people in this country. If we're panicky about Cubans, and if we think that Cubans are ten feet tall—that they are supermen and that they are going to sweep the African continent—we're in trouble. . . .
> / Andrew Young, 1978[10]

Despite the fact that Cuba has been—at a superficial level—on the sidelines of international developments for almost two decades, it has been

---

*In October 1978 Fidel Castro is quoted as having said, "We are satisfied and glad because we are nationalists. We are not only Marxist-Leninists, but also nationalists and patriots." *The International Herald Tribune,* 24 October 1978.

the recipient of its intrigues (the Missile Crisis, for one) and a participant as well as an influence in the continuing formation of world politics. As a socialist experiment and as a declared member of the Third World, it has a very special place in the ongoing debate between industrialized and nonindustrialized nations. Cuba's successful development and the ideological experimentation it has provided other countries seeking national identity have been the ingredients of Cuba's far greater impact on world socialism and world affairs than would normally have been expected from so small a nation.[11] Just as the tracking down and final murder of Che Guevara only made him a taller hero in death and captured the imagination of the young rebels of the sixties all over the world, so it appears that the Cubans' support of independence movements in Africa has made them "ten feet tall" in life. It seems, whatever else the Cuban Revolution is all about, that the Cuban experiment makes contact with an uneasy suspicion—maybe a hope—held by many people that Cuba somehow embodies a new attitude, a new spirit, a new modality in social affairs which, despite temporary successful efforts to cut it cold, signifies finally the end of international arrangements three centuries old. To understand why the Cuban "road to socialism" is such a compelling force, it is important to determine the nature of this impact. For there is no doubt that the continuing success of Cuba's transformation depends on the interplay of its international image and the way it chooses to institutionalize its revolution. Nor can there be any doubt that the way in which the West, particularly the United States, and Cuba define their relations in the future will also be so affected.

Cuba's joining the international community provokes the same mixture of admiration and worry as its victory in evolving a national community. Cuba will be confronting the full impact of a burgeoning technocratic culture nurtured by the "old politics," by both its "friends" (the Soviets) and its "enemies" (the Western bloc). There are no comfortable guidelines in the "new politics" for the Cubans to follow: the actors are not yet all in place and, although their outlook is radical, their world views are not fully articulated. The worry is that Cuba may fall prey to these uncertainties in the new politics; or be taken in by the promises of riches in technological transfers from either the West or the East and fall victim to its own miscalculations of internal strength. Already riddled with an emphasis on technical solutions, Cuba may fail to ward off the poverty of a technocratic culture.

Therefore, in thinking about the new Cuban presence in international affairs—its military action in Africa, its alliance with the Third World, its influence on socialist practice, and its renewed relations with the West—it is important to keep in mind the dialectic underlying the new politics: the affirmation or negation of the *freedom question* left unresolved by the asymmetrical development of politically democratic or undemocratic capitalisms as well as totalitarian socialisms.

To attempt to explain the current state of human affairs by way of *Realpolitik* (in academia its counterpart is "game theory") is a denial of historical process and a "cover-up" of the possibility of abrupt changes in societal organization and values—changes created by human invention in answer to people's needs in any particular historical moment.* Claims that Cuba's actions in Africa are payments for Soviet assistance, or that Cuba has always had cultural and racial ties to African societies and therefore found it "natural" to "intervene," are only rationalizations after the fact, although they may well be factors in the process. To describe, however, is not to explain. What our argument proposes is to outline a model of possible explanation and prognosis which is historical rather than behavioral, even though we are well aware that all prognosis is dangerous.

CUBA AND THE NEW MODALITIES

In the realm of rational politics, if not in the rhetoric of the Cold War, the simplistic collision theory between the capitalist and socialist worlds has long since been put aside. The life span of the Cuban Revolution is in itself a testimonial to this fact, as are its past trials and tribulations. The Communist world has split on the question of authoritarian or liberational roads to socialism. Collective agreement among Western democracies has had the same fate: their domestic and foreign affairs are circumscribed by public questioning on matters of human and civil rights, of equality and equity, and the paths of national political responses grow more varied. In the technical sphere, Western democracies are concerned with the consequences of increased population and pollution, of technocracy and bureaucracy, of the allocation of resources and the relationship between macro-planning and decentralization. People in socialist countries have the same concerns. But, despite this commonality, the once-favored prediction of international analysts that industrialization prerequisites would force an economic coherence between the "two worlds" has not come to pass. Instead, the awareness of these commonalities has made for a disquietude in the internal and international affairs of nations and for the emergence of new attitudinal modalities—expressions of the clash between

---

*No matter what our political persuasion, we have allowed some of these changes to be called "revolutions": the "agricultural revolution," the "urban revolution," the "industrial revolution," the "post-industrial revolution," etc.

"grand views" of political organization, authoritarian or liberational. The disquietude reflects the learning process which comes from a growing recognition that the different modes of producing and distributing goods and services in any given society are not the "black boxes" from which flow the "good" or "evil" human condition, and that perhaps it remains, as it always has been, a matter of people making critical political choices.

The shape of these modalities is not completely etched, but they do seem to share a common characteristic: their internal logics transcend the old-fashioned capitalist-socialist dichotomy and they redefine the play of politics and economics in their visions of the good society and the means to achieve it. The clearest differences between them are two: (1) whether they (capitalist or socialist) lean toward an elite/authoritarian or democratic/liberational form of government; and (2) whether they lean toward unequal or equal distribution systems in their internal economics. In international affairs, their clearest differences are in the connections between their policy strategies and their visions. What seem to be evolving are world views which accord different meanings to development and underdevelopment and embody different opinions as to what constitutes a "poor" or "rich" society and what social uses technology should serve. It is not that the peoples involved are anti-technical or anti-developmental. Technical know-how and increased capacity are the very growth items they want most. But in seeking ways to get them, they appear to be returning to a modern version of solving their national dilemmas in political-economy terms instead of merely "linking" politics to economic ends. The OPEC countries and Cuba are the prototypes of the consequences of this redefinition.

Of course, the modalities in the "new politics" are full of ambiguities, contradictory movements, and strange incoherences, thus the prototypes are not pure fits. It may also come to pass that these new modalities will never fully develop as powerful organizing forces. Our purpose here, however, is to point out their existence and to suggest that Cuba's future, although linked to the socialist goals, is also dependent on the political future of these emerging modalities. At present, for example, OPEC countries are generally authoritarian, theocratic, and at times monarchical. Their economies are developmental but are not based on egalitarian distribution systems. Yet included in OPEC is Venezuela, and perhaps soon there will be Mexico, two countries which have different constellations. Arab OPEC countries support the PLO, a movement supposedly Marxist in part and one which claims to be a liberational force. And, although these countries disclaim any unity with international "leftist" guerrilla movements, they on occasion train and harbor them. OPEC on the international scene demands a new economic order, a redistribution of world wealth, and therefore takes a radical stance subjecting its national economies to the larger vision of a "new politics," which seeks a change toward more equitable distributions of power and goods. The question is: Can all of this be understood as mere *Realpolitik*? Are the troubles within OPEC countries mere developmental difficulties? Are they merely the "passing of traditional society" in pain and turmoil? Is this all a "local" affair? Tribalism? Paternalism? A new hegemony as Saudi Arabia and other Muslim countries would appear to desire? OPEC, after all, represents a large part of the Third World with which Fidel Castro identifies Cuba; he sometimes castigates the OPEC members because their politics of oil hurts other Third World partners more than it does the industrialized West. OPEC is also that part of the Third World which makes contact with those forces within the nations of the so-called First and Second Worlds that see corporatism as the most viable political model for development.

Cuba, as the prototype of the other modality in the new politics, is also full of contradictions as we have already recounted: it is authoritarian in national policy decisions, allowing political participation only at middle and lower levels, but it has an egalitarian economic distribution system. Cuba on the international scene has identified itself with liberation movements on a selective basis, the criterion apparently being the "authenticity" of a movement's promise of both political and economic change, as opposed to the "anti-imperialist" claims of either reactionary nationalists or vulgar Marxists. Cuba, too, is part of the so-called Third World, but in opposition to the authoritarian modality in the new politics, Cuba's world view makes contact with those forces in the rest of the world which have come to realize the importance of "type" of political structure and that continuing abilities to be critical must accompany true democratic aims even in periods of transition. This is true despite the inconsistencies within Cuba's political structure and the lack of self-criticism on the national level. The questions here are: Can all of this be understood as merely a "local" variant of Soviet ideology? Is Cuba merely the "cat's paw" of the Soviets in the internal conflict between socialisms? Are Cuban interchanges with Latin American and African liberational struggles merely "deviations" caused by historical or cultural ties? Were the Cuban experiment's tribulations mere developmental difficulties compounded by the geographical closeness and hegemonic history of the colossus of the north? Is Cuba merely a pawn in the old politics of the Cold War? Is Cuba's desire to create the "new man" and to end her dependency simply a "dream" to coopt another world generation?

These questions and the answers to them make up some of the problematics of the new politics and of the Cuban situation. But the world views of each of the new modalities must respond also to the growing reliance on technology and science to "solve" the problems of material existence and even to impose a "scientistic" logic on human interrelations. In this sense, the new politics is an attempt to reorder priorities in terms of the actual conditions in twentieth-century societal development. It is a politics which may put a century and a half of nineteenth-century politics to bed at last. The ambiguities of the new politics are compounded by elements of historical processes not yet played out in all parts of the globe. And, as with all large-scale politics, its inconsistencies are connected to the processes of a grand view in the making. The emergence of the new politics is, I think, one more sign that we are living in another of those periods which may elicit one of those historic human inventions such as the "industrial revolution."

CHOICES AND PRESSURES

Cuba has done much in her period of near-isolation. She has developed herself, and created another role model for the nonindustrialized world, one that world cannot ignore. Although our three Aesopian morals, which summarize her answers to underdevelopment, are only developmental verities, they should not be forgotten, for they have left perhaps unintended but nevertheless troublesome legacies in Cuban society. The leaders of Cuba's Revolution claim to be Marxist-Leninists, but they also lay claim to being unique, unscarred by Old World schisms and not inevitably tied to Old World realities. Their perspective derives more from the specifics of their own culture, history, and the lessons learned in their own development. They have made Cuba a nation, and although they have made it clear that they will not quarrel with or criticize those who have given them assistance, neither will they give up the struggle to be independent.

A part of Cuba's success is due to the recognition by Cuban leaders in the late sixties that they must seriously formulate a national plan in order to rationalize Cuban priorities. The idea is not new or untried. In socialism, state planning is an instrument of transition (from old to new regime), a means to correct old inequities of class, region, and race. And, in underdeveloped countries where socialist revolutions have triumphed, state planning is the method of creating the wealth needed for self-sustaining modernization (a belief shared by nonsocialist, nonindustrialized countries as well). State planning in socialism is therefore a transitional problem, the need for which, like the State, will "wither away." At least that is the theory. National state planning is also part of the agenda in Western Europe and the United States, especially since the end of the Second World War. And, for the Western democracies also, macro-economic planning is a futuristic enterprise involving the reallocation of resources. The difference between the modalities in the "old politics"—whatever their real outcomes—lies in their definitions of the recipients of equity adjustments. It is not the factor of being highly industrialized which makes for commonality in these old modalities, but the common tendency in both to adhere to a technocratic vision of life. It is this which poses the outside danger to the liberational aspirations of many Cubans. In both of the old modalities, communist and capitalist, there is a growing belief in technical innovation and science, the source, they believe, of the hard data and expert knowledge which will provide the necessary "truth" inputs for competent macro-planning. Despite the promise of equality in these societies, there is a growing distance between those who supposedly have the knowledge—the planners—and those who are planned for—the unknowledgeable populace.

For the Cubans, who have so painfully forged a social nation and who now feel they can trade in a more diversified international market, the price tag accompanying the technological transfer they need will be the highly complicated and intense struggle to maintain their unique road to full equality internally as well as their avant-garde position in the international arena of the new politics.

The Cuban problematic, then, concerns not only how they will theoretically and in their everyday lives define their socialism, but how they will cope with the pressures which cannot help but impinge on their national life. The arsenal of weapons they have is mixed. The legacy of their development since 1959 contains an overemphasis on technical know-how to the detriment of democratic know-why, the formation of a serious and dedicated middle-management bureaucracy, and a perhaps justifiable but nevertheless pervasive fear of critical intellectuality and theoretical creativity. As we have pointed out before, the Cuban leadership cadre is not unaware of these deficits, and when asked about them, they reach for the one thing we Americans most basically share with them. The question we asked in 1974 of the two most prominent theoreticians of the Cuban politbureau was: Do you believe that Cuba might fall into a repressive personalistic dictatorship? The reply was "No"; "the Cuban people would not permit it, because of their idiosyncrasy as Cubans."[12] What Cubans seem to have —something most other peoples attempting socialism do not have, but which seems to be the motor force behind the new movement of Eurocommunism in Italy and Spain and among young people who have moved to the "spontaneous left"—is the belief in the critical capacity of their culture and people to find a way to be free. Unfortunately, this is beyond the comprehension of persons with authoritarian leanings.

If any meaning can be drawn from Cuba's developmental process, it is that, in the twentieth century, it has become evident that political choices must accompany economic ones. If Cuba's type of socialism can be placed anywhere, it is in the nub of the emerging modalities of the new politics. It is likely that the Cuban experiment will continue to have an impact in the international arena only if Cuba, together with others, continues to elaborate the liberational mode in the new politics.

Notes

1. "Castro: Russia's Cat's Paw," *Newsweek*, 12 June 1978.

2. Jorge I. Domínguez, "Cuban Foreign Policy," *Foreign Affairs* 57, no. 1 (Fall 1978).

3. For a more complete discussion of this emphatic emphasis, see Marlis Krueger and Frieda Silvert, *Dissent Denied* (New York: Elsevier, 1975).

4. "Andrew Young on Africa: Still the Voice of Dissent," *Newsweek*, 12 June 1978.

5. *Ibid.*

6. Domínguez, "Cuban Foreign Policy."

7. Herbert Matthews, *Revolution in Cuba* (New York: Charles Scribner's Sons, 1975).

8. For a complete and measured analysis of the Carter administration's policy in Latin America, see Abraham F. Lowenthal, "Latin America: A Not-So-Special Relationship," *Foreign Policy*, no. 32 (Fall 1978).

9. In "Castro: Russia's Cat's Paw," cited earlier.

10. "Andrew Young on Africa," cited earlier.

11. Domínguez, "Cuban Foreign Policy."

12. Silvert and Silvert, "Fate, Chance, and Faith," in *Essays in Understanding Latin America*, p. 94.

Cuba's Sugar Policy

G. B. HAGELBERG

There was a saying in Cuba before the revolution that summed up the dominant role of the sugar industry: *Sin azúcar, no hay país* (without sugar, there is no country). The fact that this aphorism is almost as apposite today as it was twenty or even fifty years ago points to a historical constant amid all the changes wrought by the Cuban Revolution. Indeed, a bird's-eye view of the Cuban sugar scene discloses a number of familiar landmarks; but like old buildings surviving in a reconstructed city, they bear a changed relationship to their surroundings and have undergone interior alteration.

The growing and processing of sugar cane is still Cuba's leading industry, and sugar remains the principal export commodity. According to official Cuban statistics, sugar exports in 1974—admittedly a year of record prices in the world market—brought in 1.92 thousand million pesos, 86.4 percent of the total value of exports and triple the 1971 figure on roughly the same volume. Thanks to the high returns from sugar, Cuba's trade balance in 1974 for the first time in many years showed only a negligible deficit. On this happy note, Banco Nacional de Cuba invited several hundred foreign bankers, from every major country except the United States, to Havana for the celebration of its twenty-fifth anniversary in October 1975, and the guests reciprocated the entertainment with a five-year Euroloan for 350 million German marks. *La danza de los millones* is a recurring event in Cuban history; unfortunately, the dance never lasts very long. By 1976 the precipitous decline of world sugar prices from their 1974 peak was forcing cutbacks in the 1976–80 economic plan and a general belt-tightening.

The volume of Cuban sugar production and exports has recovered from the slump of the 1960s, but it began to rise appreciably above the

31

Table 1 / Cuban Sugar Production, Exports, Consumption and
Stocks, 1950–76 (Metric Tons, Raw Value)

Calendar Year	Production	Exports	Consumption	Stocks at End of Year
1950	5,557,505	5,260,810	247,394	296,320
1951	5,759,145	5,441,633	292,015	291,926
1952	7,224,539	5,007,728	302,614	2,164,705
1953	5,159,172	5,516,334	257,600	1,485,004
1954	4,890,439	4,226,108	206,080	1,942,838
1955	4,527,621	4,644,095	206,080	1,620,283
1956	4,740,414	5,394,220	312,454	637,525
1957	5,671,915	5,307,022	303,725	680,684
1958	5,783,726	5,631,592	241,795	547,342
1959	5,964,113	4,951,874	331,061	1,222,033
1960	5,861,800	5,634,513	347,491	1,096,961
1961	6,767,034	6,413,561	376,000	1,030,000
1962	4,815,234	5,130,940	373,094	341,200
1963	3,821,070	3,520,505	455,987	185,778
1964	4,589,506	4,176,051	401,450	197,783
1965	6,082,158	5,315,630	492,351	471,960
1966	4,866,710	4,434,639	541,529	362,502
1967	6,236,000	5,682,872	629,498	286,132
1968	5,315,197	4,612,923	681,613*	306,793
1969	5,534,180	4,798,817	636,298*	405,858
1970	7,558,569	6,906,286	619,376*	438,765
1971	5,950,029	5,510,860	616,089*	261,845
1972	4,687,802	4,139,556	470,890	339,201
1973	5,382,548	4,797,377	463,742	460,630
1974	5,925,850	5,491,247	522,162	373,071
1975	6,427,382	5,743,711	499,313	557,429
1976	6,150,797	5,763,652	531,919	412,655

*Of which for animal feeding: 1968—20,052 tons; 1969—93,994 tons; 1970—
85,338 tons; 1971—53,587 tons.

Source: International Sugar Council (1963:II); International Sugar Council/Or-
ganization (1956ff.).

level of the early 1950s only in the last two years for which data are available. When annual fluctuations (see Table 1) are averaged out, volumes have changed remarkably little after a quarter of a century:

Years	Production (metric tons)	Index	Exports (metric tons)	Index
1950–54	5,718,160	100	5,090,523	100
1955–59	5,337,558	93	5,185,761	102
1960–64	5,170,929	90	4,975,114	98
1965–69	5,606,849	98	4,968,976	98
1970–74	5,900,960	103	5,369,065	105
1975–76	6,289,090	110	5,753,682	113

The problems of Cuban sugar statistics have been discussed elsewhere (Hagelberg 1974:53–60);* these figures should be taken only as approximations. In particular, comparisons of the performance of the Cuban sugar industry at different times must make allowance for the production and export of high-test molasses before the revolution, which represented an alternative form of sugar cane utilization developed in the 1930s as a result of the imposition of marketing restrictions on sugar. Inclusion of the raw sugar equivalent of high-test molasses would, on average, increase the production and export figures for the 1950s by about 200,000 metric tons a year (Hagelberg 1974:132) and would shift the index figures constructed on the 1950–54 base by about two points.

While output has remained much the same, the island's population has grown. As a result, per capita annual production, which reached about one ton of sugar per inhabitant in the first half of the 1950s, has declined by one-third, back to the pre-World War II level. In the international league of centrifugal sugar producers Cuba has dropped from first to fourth place, behind the Soviet Union, Brazil, and the United States; or to fifth place, if the European Economic Community (EEC) is considered a unit. Cuba's share in world pro-

*A difficulty not alluded to there is the secrecy surrounding the Cuban sugar industry in the last fifteen years. While Cuba is not alone in treating as classified information the data relating to this prosaic commodity—and, given the role of sugar production in its economy, has perhaps more excuse than others—it is probably the only country where such reticence is considered to confer a tangible economic benefit. According to the Cuban sugar journal *ATAC* (36 [no. 1/1977]:22), a four-day seminar on state secrets in the sugar sector was held in December 1976 under the chairmanship of the Minister of the Sugar Industry. A photograph of the event shows a banner, stretched across the wall behind the presiding functionaries, which bears the legend: "The protection of state secrets is our contribution to the economy."

duction fell from about 17 percent at the beginning of the 1950s to roughly 7 percent in 1976. This inevitably means that Cuba has lost some of its ability to influence world sugar affairs.

With average annual exports in excess of 5 million metric tons, however, Cuba is still the largest sugar exporter in the world, accounting for approximately one-quarter of world exports in the most recent period. Comparisons with earlier years are not meaningful in this case because of structural changes, above all the exclusion from world export statistics of shipments within the EEC, which are now regarded as internal movements.

In addition to the unchanged quantities, the structural and institutional features of Cuba's sugar trade also exhibit a certain continuity, at least superficially. This is due to the fact that Cuba's sugar exports do not stand on their own but rather are intimately connected with its overall political-economic orientation. The "special arrangement" (cf. Chapter IX of the International Sugar Agreement of 1977) with the country's principal foreign ally to provide a guaranteed outlet for a large part of the crop and a shelter against the volatility of free-world market prices continues to be the cornerstone of Cuba's sugar economy. Although changed in substance, it has been preserved as an institution of Cuba's sugar policy—the erstwhile partner, the United States, being replaced after 1960 by the Soviet Union and the other socialist countries.

From this derives the continued geographical concentration of Cuban sugar exports that is another persistent aspect of the island's sugar situation. In the period 1950–59, the United States received 46–59 percent of Cuban sugar exports (Table 2). Since 1961, at least 56.5 percent of Cuban sugar sales in any one year have been to the socialist countries, the minimum share of the Soviet Union alone being 26.5 percent.

Enumeration of the elements common to the pre- and postrevolutionary periods serves to outline the limits within which Cuban policy makers have had to operate and within which their decisions may reasonably be evaluated. They could and did nationalize foreign properties and transfer the entire sugar complex, with the exception of small cane growers, to the public sector. They could and did alter the supply of the factors of production, which among other things unexpectedly provoked an acute shortage of labor during harvests and hastened the need for machines to cut and load cane, in the midst of an economic blockade and at a time when there was yet little international experience in sugar cane mechanization. They could and did change marketing procedures so that the greater part of Cuban sugar exports is now negotiated between state agencies in Cuba and those in the importing nations within the framework of intergovernmental economic agreements (a development to which the change in trading partners also contributed, of course). But they could not endow the country with a new set of resources, and they had to come to terms eventually with the facts that Cuba is a relatively small open economy, heavily dependent on foreign trade for both maintenance and development, and that agricultural diversification is a very slow process. The circumstances that dictated the renewed emphasis on sugar production in 1963 and the attempt to expand sugar exports have been sufficiently discussed to be taken as known (e.g., Boorstein 1968; Matthews 1969:150; Castro 1970a, 1970b). There can be little doubt that conceptually this was the correct response to the economic problems facing the country, although the obstacles in the way of increasing sugar production and, above all, of stabilizing it at the higher level to meet long-range export commitments, were in turn seriously underestimated.

From Table 1 it can be seen that both production and exports have been subject to wide annual fluctuations which are lost in the five-year averages cited earlier. As a matter of fact, output has been even more variable than is indicated by these figures, which are given by calendar year and in recent years take in parts of two crops, since the beginning of the harvest has been brought forward. Calculated on a crop-year basis, the last nine *zafras* (crops) have ranged between a low of 4.4 million metric tons in 1971/72 and a high of 8.5 million tons in 1969/70; there is some indication, however, that the fluctuations are becoming less violent.

The irregularity of production is directly reflected in the volume of exports since the buffers that used to separate the two have been dismantled. Table 1 shows that after 1961 year-end stocks have been held down to less than 10 percent of annual exports. The other reserve that existed in the 1950s and which could be used to make up for poor yields—leftover cane—was eliminated at the same time. Citing statistics of the Empresa Consolidada del Azúcar, Bernardo (1963) reported that the area of cane held over from the previous crop was reduced from some 220,000 hectares (16.4 percent of the total area available for harvesting) in 1961 to about 65,000 hectares (5.6 percent) in 1963. From that year on, as far as is known, the crop has consisted (with the possible exception of the 1969/70 harvest) almost entirely of ratoons (new shoots springing from the cane stool after reaping) and whatever new cane was planted in time to be fit for cutting; the crop has therefore been all the more susceptible to variation because of climatic conditions. To be sure, artificial irrigation capabilities have increased substantially, but they evidently do not yet compensate sufficiently for lack of rainfall. With no sizable reserves of either standing cane in the

Table 2 / *Centrifugal Sugar Exports of Cuba by Major Destination, 1950–76 (Metric Tons, Raw Value)*

Year	United States	Percentage	U.S.S.R.	Percentage	Other socialist countries*	Percentage	Other countries	Percentage
1950	2,873,131	54.6	0	0	0	0	2,387,679	45.4
1951	2,634,135	48.4	0	0	0	0	2,807,498	51.6
1952	2,664,203	53.2	0	0	0	0	2,343,525	46.8
1953	2,529,509	45.9	9,606	0.2	0	0	2,977,219	54.0
1954	2,410,040	57.0	9,506	0.2	0	0	1,806,562	42.7
1955	2,574,083	55.4	456,379	9.8	29,011	0.6	1,584,622	34.1
1956	2,812,744	52.1	212,624	3.9	56,857	1.1	2,311,995	42.9
1957	2,785,497	52.5	358,242	6.8	28,423	0.5	2,134,860	40.2
1958	3,241,374	57.6	187,683	3.3	63,723	1.1	2,138,812	38.0
1959	2,987,216	59.3	273,776	5.5	0	0	1,740,882	35.2
1960	1,948,574	34.6	1,577,683	28.0	703,225	12.5	1,405,031	24.9
1961	0	0	3,302,865	51.5	1,522,422	23.7	1,588,274	24.8
1962	0	0	2,112,245	41.2	1,631,227	31.8	1,387,468	27.0
1963	0	0	973,423	27.7	1,106,087	31.4	1,440,995	40.9
1964	0	0	1,936,798	46.4	724,073	17.3	1,515,180	36.3
1965	0	0	2,456,144	46.2	1,154,201	21.7	1,705,285	32.1
1966	0	0	1,814,930	40.9	1,442,729	32.5	1,176,980	26.5
1967	0	0	2,473,305	43.5	1,457,356	25.6	1,752,211	30.8
1968	0	0	1,831,727	39.7	1,368,187	29.7	1,413,009	30.6
1969	0	0	1,352,329	28.2	1,523,006	31.7	1,923,482	40.1

(continued on next page)

Table 2 (Continued)

Year	United States	Percentage	U.S.S.R.	Percentage	Other socialist countries*	Percentage	Other countries	Percentage
1970	0	0	3,105,030	45.0	1,696,959	24.6	2,104,297	30.5
1971	0	0	1,580,988	28.7	1,769,745	32.1	2,160,127	39.2
1972	0	0	1,097,406	26.5	1,240,683	30.0	1,801,467	43.5
1973	0	0	1,660,681	34.6	1,362,705	28.4	1,773,991	37.0
1974	0	0	1,974,761	36.0	1,342,147	24.4	2,174,339	39.6
1975	0	0	3,186,724	55.5	904,626	15.7	1,652,361	28.8
1976	0	0	3,035,566	52.7	1,344,498	23.3	1,383,498	24.0

*Albania, Bulgaria, China, Czechoslovakia, German Democratic Republic, Hungary, Mongolia, North Korea, North Vietnam, Poland, Romania, Yugoslavia (cf. Article 36, International Sugar Agreement of 1968).

Source: International Sugar Council/Organization (1956ff.).

field or sugar in the warehouse, Cuban sugar marketing has become very much a hand-to-mouth affair.

There is every reason to believe that the fluctuations in output largely violated the design of the policy makers, and there is no evidence to suggest that they were produced intentionally, either in response to, or in an attempt to influence, price movements on the world market. The long-term trade agreement between Cuba and the Soviet Union, concluded early in 1964, set targets for Cuban sugar exports to that country rising from 2.1 million tons in 1965 to 5 million tons yearly in 1968–70. In accordance with this agreement, the sugar planners postulated a step-by-step increase in production from 6 to 10 million tons (Castro 1970a).

Without conducting another post-mortem of the 1969/70 harvest, which has been eloquently criticized by the Cuban leaders themselves, let me point out that the plan guided itself naively by historical averages with little attention to measures of dispersion. In the event, cane and sugar yields in the period 1964–70 (which excludes the extremely low yields registered in 1963) had a range of 37.1–55.7 tons/hectare and 4.5–6.0 tons/hectare, respectively, the highest cane yield being achieved in 1970 and the highest sugar yield in 1967 (Hagelberg 1974: 143).

Large year-to-year changes in yields constitute one of the reasons for the observed instability in output. The other reason is variations in the area harvested, which ranged from a low of 938,000 hectares in 1969 to 1,455,000 hectares in 1970. Here again there is scant evidence of willful manipulation. The low figure in 1969 does invite the suspicion that cane was being saved for the big show in 1970, and a large harvest in the Soviet Union in 1969 allowed that country to appear as a net exporter, rendering the need for Cuban sugar in that quarter less urgent. Neither factor, however, is likely to have played a major role. Taking into account plantings of new cane in previous years and the natural attrition among ratoons, it rather seems that not much more cane was fit for harvesting in 1969. There can also be little doubt that the effort of having simultaneously to carry out the 1969 *zafra* and to make preparations for the one in 1970 put a strain on resources and organizational capacity.

The performance since 1970 tends to support this analysis. Some retrenchment from the record achieved in 1969/70 was to be anticipated in view of the extraordinary social costs of the crusade to reach 10 million tons—the dislocations experienced in other sectors of the Cuban economy. But the delay in getting back to a growth trend, notwithstanding the improvement in prices, also points to unresolved organizational problems. The drop to 4.4 million tons in 1971/72 was foreshadowed by the decline in new plantings in 1970. There are various indications that the 1971/72 crop represented a low point in efficiency and that performance has since tended to improve, although the *zafra* of 1974/75 was again said to have been affected by drought (Vázquez 1974; Dorticós 1974). A basic prerequisite to stabilizing Cuban sugar production on a higher level is the capacity to replace old cane at an adequate rate year after year. If, however, we are to take literally the statement made by President Dorticós in a speech to sugar workers in October 1974 that the five-year plan for 1976–80 aimed to raise production "not by sudden jumps but through steady year-by-year growth" —which was also the aim of the sugar plan of 1965–70—a reserve of either standing cane or sugar to even out the inevitable yield fluctuations would be required. Standing cane would probably be the most economic stabilizer and could be used alternatively as livestock feed or to produce alcohol.

Since the aggressive selling in 1960–61 reduced stocks to a level where the quantity available for export was directly related to the level of production, which Cuban policy makers were unable to stabilize, the irregularity of total exports must be largely unrelated to market conditions. The only doubtful point here is the great increase in apparent consumption in 1967–71, which still puzzles foreign observers (see Table 1). Even after deducting the quantities destined for animal feeding, the per capita levels of human sugar consumption indicated by these figures are quite incredible. But at most an additional 200,000 tons could have been made available for export from the consumption column. The diversion of sugar to animal feed ceased in 1972 when world market prices rose sharply, and this is the only instance of apparent response to market conditions to be noted in the global figures in Table 1.

A breakdown of Cuban sugar exports by major destination is provided in Table 2. Up to 1960, Cuba had the largest quota of any foreign country selling to the United States. In the period 1955–59 it furnished on average 2,870,000 metric tons, raw value, of centrifugal sugar annually, equivalent to over 70 percent of all foreign centrifugal sugar entering the United States (International Sugar Council 1963:II, 165f.), in addition to quantities of high-test molasses and liquid sugar. The U.S. import duty on Cuban sugar was 0.5 cents per pound of sugar, 96° polarization, against 0.625 cents for full-duty countries. Monthly prices in this period fluctuated between 4.87 and 5.68 cents per pound of sugar in bags f.a.s. Cuba (International Sugar Council 1963:II, 181). Following the cessation of the sugar trade between Cuba and the United States in 1960, the Soviet Union (already in the 1950s an occasional buyer of Cuban sugar in substantial amounts), China, and several East European countries in effect substituted for the American market.

This accommodation was all the more remarkable because Eastern Europe presented no natural outlet for Cuban sugar at that point. Czechoslovakia and Poland were and still are net exporters every year (disregarding the exceptional lapse of Czechoslovakia into the net-importer column in 1976); Bulgaria was a net exporter from 1955 to 1960, East Germany with interruptions until 1964, Hungary continuously from 1959 to 1969, and Romania from 1960 to 1969 and again in 1972–73 (International Sugar Council/Organization 1956ff.). An excellent harvest in Cuba in 1961 provided enough sugar to raise total exports to a record level, not surpassed until 1970, and the amount purchased by the socialist countries in 1961 in fact greatly exceeded the amount previously purchased by the United States in any one year. To a lesser extent this was also true in 1962, but at the expense of Cuba's sugar reserves and with smaller exports to other (nonsocialist) countries.

Since 1962, Cuban exports to the Soviet Union have ranged from less than 1 million tons in 1963 to more than 3 million tons in 1970, 1975, and 1976, while exports to the other socialist countries registered a low point in 1964 with some 720,000 tons and a high point in 1971 with close to 1,770,000 tons. In comparison, Cuba's sugar exports to other countries have been relatively stable, moving within a range of about 1.2–2.2 million tons.

The trade with the Soviet Union thus bore the brunt of the fluctuation in quantity of sugar available for export. Cuba was evidently concerned, in the first place, with satisfying the demand from other quarters, particularly its export entitlements under the International Sugar Agreement of 1968. To be sure, Cuban exports to nonsocialist countries reached a low point in 1966, coincident with the low point in free-world market prices, while the socialist bloc was supplied relatively more generously out of the poor harvest that year. But on the whole Cuba's performance contrasts with that of other Caribbean producers in this respect. It is the only Caribbean sugar exporter to have exposed itself without interruption to the vagaries of the free market and to have regularly offered a substantial portion of its output to buyers at world market prices, high or low. Unlike the other Caribbean producers that had quotas under the U.S. Sugar Act or the Commonwealth Sugar Agreement, Cuba evidently could not regard the free market as a residual outlet but had to give it priority in order to earn convertible currency since its special arrangements with the socialist countries were based essentially on barter.

The Soviet Union has repeatedly raised the accounting price put on Cuban sugar in these transactions. At the end of 1972 it was agreed to roughly double the 6-cent level that ruled throughout the 1960s; in 1974, the price is understood to have been increased to the equivalent of about 20 cents per pound; and in October 1975 it was announced that for the period 1975–80 the price had been fixed at the equivalent of about 30 cents per pound. In light of the record it seems reasonable to suggest that these moves were motivated not only by a desire to help Cuba and to keep up with the trend of world market prices but also by Russia's need to assure for itself a larger and more constant share of Cuba's sugar exports. It is not clear to what extent Cuba's other socialist trading partners have followed the Soviet lead on pricing. The price announced for Soviet sugar purchases in the period 1975–80 bears no relation to probable costs of production in Cuba and, leaving aside the peak year 1974, does not reflect average world market values. From various Cuban statements it appears that the price of Cuban sugar delivered to the Soviet Union from 1975 on was determined by reference to the prices put by that country on its exports to Cuba and thus may be taken to represent a form of indexation, the implication being that the sugar price may rise even higher than 30 cents per pound if the prices of Soviet goods are increased. In any event, it is increasingly difficult to analyze Cuba's sugar trade with the Soviet Union in isolation from the broader context of its economic and political relations with that country.

Table 3 shows the distribution of Cuban sugar within the socialist bloc. After the Soviet Union, China has been the major customer, followed by the German Democratic Republic. Whether as an accommodation to Cuba or for other reasons, production in most Eastern European countries has tended to stagnate or decline in recent years. This, together with large increases in consumption (which in some cases includes sugar actually exported in manufactured food products such as fruit preserves), by the end of the 1960s had created substantial outlets for Cuban sugar where none existed at the beginning of the decade. Noteworthy, too, is the growth of shipments to North Korea and Vietnam, although deliveries to the former show a sharp decline in 1974–1976.

In fact, world sugar movements indicate that since 1971 Cuba has been unable to cover fully the requirements of its socialist trading partners who in 1972, 1973, and again in 1976 made large purchases on the world market (Table 4) which they surely would have avoided had Cuban sugar been available. Incomplete data for 1977 show exports from the Philippines alone of 655,714 metric tons, raw value, to

Table 3 / Cuban Sugar Exports to Socialist Countries, Except U.S.S.R., by Country of Destination, 1960–76 (Metric Tons, Raw Value; Continued on Next Page)

Year	Albania	Bulgaria	China	Czechoslovakia	G.D.R.	Hungary
1960	0	0	476,537	8,988	61,867	0
1961	0	57,258	1,032,136	25,322	111,910	0
1962	10,700	117,796	937,893	155,680	179,343	0
1963	6,419	56,177	500,928	150,105	244,490	0
1964	10,810	87,248	386,352	52,071	81,054	0
1965	11,297	157,692	398,216	244,618	169,878	0
1966	10,490	158,051	619,731	262,098	207,192	0
1967	4,235	194,671	556,079	214,884	249,623	16,730
1968	17,098	186,431	431,108	193,490	243,656	16,574
1969	0	205,308	444,554	224,356	252,508	16,663
1970	10,807	231,170	530,430	226,605	352,666	16,304
1971	23,278	210,655	463,947	189,638	338,096	59,396
1972	15,108	154,257	295,176	151,132	243,028	38,069
1973	13,855	212,634	302,030	163,018	259,488	52,422
1974	12,850	190,144	358,670	160,484	276,003	51,369
1975	14,171	185,728	182,877	55,745	169,195	41,762
1976	13,169	232,042	254,315	109,172	194,868	70,007

Source: International Sugar Council/Organization (1956ff.).

the Soviet Union and of 277,418 tons to China, while Thailand shipped 674,338 tons, tel quel, to China.

Although these figures indicate that Cuba's socialist trading partners could absorb additional quantities of Cuban sugar if they were available, there has been considerable speculation in international sugar circles since the beginning of 1977 concerning a possible inconsistency between the Cuban and Russian plans for the expansion of their respective sugar industries (cf. Foreign Agriculture, 17 January 1977; F. O. Licht's International Sugar Report, 13 April 1977). Cuba's target is to produce 8–8.7 million metric tons of sugar, raw value, in 1980, while the Soviet Union plans to reach 11.2 million tons of white sugar from domestic beet (equivalent to 12.2 million tons, raw value, its largest crop to date having been of the order of 10 million tons, raw value). Read in conjunction with the planned per capita consumption level and population projections for 1980, this implies a net Soviet import requirement of only 300,000 tons. Even if the Russian plan were to be fulfilled, larger amounts of Cuban sugar could, of course, be imported, either for stockpiling or re-export. But the latter option

Table 3 (Continued)

Year	Mongolia	North Korea	Vietnam	Poland	Romania	Yugoslavia
1960	0	0	0	143,990	0	11,843
1961	0	0	0	261,927	0	33,869
1962	0	14,038	10,490	151,285	0	54,002
1963	0	20,000	13,373	103,895	0	10,700
1964	0	21,051	10,542	32,148	0	42,797
1965	0	21,458	65,997	0	0	85,045
1966	0	21,335	13,077	52,843	0	97,912
1967	5,273	83,346	45,510	22,327	0	64,678
1968	5,193	74,910	49,777	20,713	53,552	75,685
1969	0	154,851	60,129	28,134	69,143	67,360
1970	0	149,110	56,512	24,177	99,178	0
1971	0	196,704	76,106	30,313	109,312	72,300
1972	10,739	119,233	75,633	22,247	72,583	43,478
1973	2,670	135,576	75,910	55,124	78,174	11,804
1974	2,702	55,305	78,018	28,278	77,953	50,371
1975	2,698	50,441	86,918	43,100	11,224	60,767
1976	2,083	21,999	124,538	16,642	39,303	266,360

is likely to be restricted by the International Sugar Agreement, which at present limits Soviet sugar exports to the free-world market to 500,000 tons per year. Thus, in the event that Russian targets were met, it is not clear how imports from Cuba of the magnitude of its 1975–76 deliveries or larger would be accommodated.

Mention of Russian re-exports of Cuban sugar to the free market raises further questions concerning the effect of this trade on the volume of and earnings from Cuba's direct sales to that market. Although on balance a net importer (except in 1969), the Soviet Union was also a large exporter in the 1960s and up to the end of 1971. The consequences for Cuba of Russian dealings on the free market are difficult to gauge. On the one hand, it can be argued that the Soviet Union acted as a distributor for Cuban sugar insofar as it sold to countries (such as Afghanistan, Jordan, Kuwait, and Saudi Arabia) which Cuba might not have been able to reach directly. On the other hand, it must be remembered that whereas Russian imports in this period were made by special arrangement with Cuba outside the free-world market, Russian exports were directed to that market and affected its prices. Cheap

Table 4 / Centrifugal Sugar Imports by Socialist Countries from Nonsocialist Sources, 1971–76 (Metric Tons, Raw Value)

Importing country	1971	1972	1973	1974	1975	1976
Albania	0	0	6,739	0	n.a.	0
Bulgaria	0	0	0	0	95,902	97,958
China	0	453,816	433,818	51,892	58,181	372,870
G.D.R.	19,500	95,667[a]	515	0	0	5,442
Hungary	53,859	73,370	92,939	81,828	103,527	83,400
Romania	0	22	0	0	32,753	n.a.
U.S.S.R.	0	611,098	896,991	0	272,274	528,809
Vietnam, Soc. Rep.	0	0	0	50,000	151,914	84,570
Yugoslavia	39,022[b]	170,617[b]	248,597[b]	13,688[b]	57,410[b]	78,822
Total	115,774	1,419,426	1,701,216	198,598	776,953	1,251,871

[a]Includes 8,028 tons for nonhuman consumption.

[b]Refined sugar. Converted to raw value for purposes of totaling at the rate of 92 to 100 parts.

Source: International Sugar Council/Organization (1956ff.).

white sugar from Eastern Europe, offered at times at a price below that of Cuban raw, had a depressing effect on free market prices in 1967 and 1968, thus reducing Cuban earnings from that source. It is possible, of course, that greater availabilities directly from Cuba would have had the same effect, but it is also possible that Havana would have adopted a different marketing strategy.

More speculation has been generated by recent reports from Cuba of a COMECON (Council for Mutual Economic Assistance) agreement to stabilize Eastern European beet sugar production at its present level and to cover future increments in demand by imports from Cuba. This does not coincide with the announced intentions of most Eastern European countries to expand their sugar industries. While it is fairly improbable that Cuban, Soviet, and Eastern European expansion plans will all be punctually fulfilled, these apparent inconsistencies illustrate the continuing difficulty of coordinating the development of the sugar production capabilities of the various COMECON members with the growth of demand in their respective countries.

Japan has been by far the most important outlet for Cuban sugar outside the socialist bloc (Table 5), although its purchases dropped sharply in 1975 and are unlikely to regain their former level in the foreseeable future. Together with Spain, Japan accounted for nearly

70 percent of Cuban sugar sales to capitalist countries in 1974. But whereas Cuban exports to Japan were not matched by imports of similar value from that country, Cuba's exports to Spain are illustrative of its commerce with a number of other countries: they took place within the framework of trade agreements which generally included a barter provision. For example, Cuban sugar exports to Spain in 1965 were reported in trade circles to have been negotiated at a nominal price of £53.70 per ton (including cost and freight) at a time when the London Daily Price stood at around £23, but payment was to involve Spanish goods. At one time or another, Cuba has also entered into barter deals with Chile, Syria, and Uruguay. A trade agreement concluded between Cuba and Morocco in 1961 involving 150,000 tons of sugar was said to provide for the establishment of a clearing account and for payment to be made two-thirds in Moroccan goods and one-third in convertible currency. Subsequent agreements varied the proportions of free currency and clearing account payment. Table 5 shows that sales to Morocco have fluctuated since 1971, and Cuba was reduced from the largest supplier to third place in 1973 and 1974, behind Brazil and the Dominican Republic, before recovering its position in 1975. Similarly Syria, which for a number of years obtained all or most of its sugar imports from Cuba, in 1974 and 1975 bought more from Brazil.

Most of the countries listed in Table 5 were already regular markets for Cuban sugar before the revolution. Other cases, however, show the effects of changing political winds. South Korea and South Vietnam ceased to be markets for Cuban sugar in 1960 and 1961, respectively, and were replaced by North Korea and North Vietnam. Aside from negligible quantities in 1970–72, no Cuban sugar exports to West Germany have been recorded since 1962. Exports to Chile were re-established in 1971, after a five-year hiatus, only to be interrupted again in 1974. On the other hand, Portugal, which last appeared as a buyer of Cuban sugar in 1965, returned to the list in 1974. Occasional small shipments to Honduras, Panama, and Venezuela since 1972 reflect the rapprochement with Latin America. Overall, the composition of Table 5, which covers the bulk of sugar exports to nonsocialist countries, confirms that the attempt to isolate Cuba economically after the revolution had relatively little impact on its sugar sales to traditional outlets outside the United States. By the same token, Cuba is shown to have had only partial success in developing genuinely new markets for its sugar outside the socialist bloc.

More fundamentally, the pattern of Cuba's sugar exports is characterized by a high degree of compartmentalization. Not only is there the division between socialist outlets (constituting preferential markets

Table 5 / Cuban Sugar Exports to Selected Nonsocialist Countries, 1960–76 (Metric Tons, Raw Value; Continued on Next Page)

Year	Canada	Egypt	Iraq	Japan	Malaysia	Morocco
1960	74,970	108,114	22,155	204,559	0	160,986
1961	15,822	150,160	34,933	423,256	0	157,287
1962	19,880	105,112	17,991	431,482	0	265,124
1963	70,068	78,115	36,711	160,771	0	285,028
1964	3,268	95,284	0	345,582	0	323,259
1965	68,614	126,168	126,313	415,215	0	182,209
1966	69,378	97,038	0	359,961	0	181,327
1967	66,175	114,278	42,095	542,127	118,989	152,768
1968	46,739	65,599	53,124	555,422	0	85,635
1969	79,900	68,720	21,795	1,017,689	104,938	175,760
1970	65,411	31,689	21,286	1,220,941	214,536	106,035
1971	73,367	42,590	52,117	912,234	140,551	165,312
1972	31,125	21,342	55,528	909,381	87,691	55,204
1973	46,681	5,172	0	984,558	29,223	61,757
1974	115,669	0	65,162	1,151,981	64,222	40,793
1975	156,192	13,699	78,395	338,825	0	100,280
1976	149,041	23,006	83,003	149,941	18,861	108,777

Source: International Sugar Council/Organization (1956ff.).

or special arrangements in the terminology of the International Sugar Agreement) and capitalist purchasers on the free-world market; each category is further subdivided: the socialist into COMECON and non-COMECON, the capitalist into cash sales and barter. Although it is impossible to say how much convertible currency Cuban sugar brings in, since reports of possible Soviet payments in convertible currency are fragmentary and contradictory, it is certain that tied sales account for the greater part of the exports.

Cuba's position as the largest sugar supplier to the free-world market gives it a leading voice in the International Sugar Organization, the body administering the International Sugar Agreement. Following a period during the 1960s in which Cuba furnished only a minimum of statistics—and that with great delay—to what was then the International Sugar Council, of which it nevertheless continued to be a member, Cuban representatives played an active role in the organization during the life of the International Sugar Agreement of 1968. A Cuban delegate presided over the Statistics Committee in 1971, and for a while

Table 5 (Continued)

Year	Spain	Sweden	Syria	United Kingdom	Percentage[b]
1960	33,247	8,458	67,350	173,368	60.7
1961	53,208	805	—[a]	79,382	57.6
1962	58,312	28,232	50,478	76,143	75.9
1963	102,737	15,243	20,666	173,698	65.4
1964	275,704	10,721	30,961	94,144	77.8
1965	173,771	42,399	62,167	113,237	76.8
1966	145,343	44,741	53,309	61,646	86.0
1967	158,581	22,223	63,789	70,290	77.1
1968	175,678	40,893	64,133	20,065	78.4
1969	181,577	10,177	87,217	42,912	93.1
1970	143,401	60,323	97,959	0	93.2
1971	81,881	47,307	115,995	50,603	77.9
1972	97,702	64,561	101,147	28,848	80.6
1973	103,522	56,308	106,754	121,880	85.4
1974	363,127	50,818	41,311	70,951	90.3
1975	326,523	35,252	52,794	16,671	67.7
1976	114,519	108,291	106,222	138,756	72.3

[a]Included under Egypt.

[b]Total exports to the selected countries listed in this table as a percentage of all exports to "other countries" in Table 2.

official Cuban data were published more promptly. Raúl León Torras, Cuba's chief representative, was elected vice-chairman of the International Sugar Organization for 1972 and succeeded to the chairmanship in 1973, the year in which a new International Sugar Agreement for the period 1974–78 was to be negotiated in a conference under the auspices of the United Nations at Geneva.

In an interview prior to the conference (Vázquez 1973a), León Torras assumed the role of spokesman of the exporting members of the International Sugar Organization, particularly the economically less developed ones. Cuba in fact came to play that role in the negotiations (the then First Deputy Minister of Cuba's Ministry of Foreign Trade was elected first vice-chairman of the Geneva conference as representative of the exporters). But the 1973 conference failed because no agreement could be reached between exporters and importers, especially on the question of prices. The only thing to emerge was an administrative agreement to maintain the International Sugar Organization as an information-gathering and consultative body without regulatory functions.

In a subsequent interview (Vázquez 1973b), the leader of the Cuban delegation, Marcelo Fernández Font, Minister for Foreign Trade, blamed the failure of the conference on the intransigence of the importing countries. While he thought the 1968 agreement had fulfilled its objectives, it had been made obsolete by the intervening changes in volume and price. When he came to express Cuba's continuing interest in arriving at a new regulatory instrument, Fernández Font stressed several times what is probably the guiding principle of Cuba's sugar policy:

> In the long run, our country is interested in the existence of a Sugar Agreement that establishes remunerative prices for sugar and limits production and exports of other countries. . . .
>
> Looking several years ahead, it could indeed be detrimental for our country if there were no regulatory mechanism in the world market.

And again:

> Seen in perspective, the nonexistence of a Sugar Agreement would permit the expansion of output of the producing and exporting countries which, in practice, would be Cuba's competitors. This is why it would be convenient for our country to have once again in the future a market-regulating instrument, a new Agreement.

Indeed, this was and still is the basic dilemma—how to get satisfactory prices and still discourage the competition. It has been very much exacerbated by Cuba's own experience of rising production costs (Hagelberg 1974:66–67) in the years since 1960, when the late Raúl Cepero Bonilla, then Cuba's Minister for Trade, stated in a television appearance that his country was opposed to prices in the four-cent range because they encouraged marginal production. Three-cent prices, he reasoned, would not prove unhealthy for the island in the long run.

It is probably because this dilemma is really insoluble—Cuba having left the ranks of the low-cost producers—that Cuba supported formation of the Group of Latin American and Caribbean Sugar Exporting Countries (GEPLACEA), which met for the first time in Mexico in November 1974. The reserve with which Fernández Font in 1973 had treated the idea of unilateral action by the exporting countries was swept aside. A Cuban official became the first executive secretary of the new association, which has as its basic objective "to serve as a flexible

consulting and coordinating mechanism for the common matters related to the production and marketing of sugar." Cuba's change of
position notwithstanding, it is doubtful whether, given the characteristics of the world sugar economy, such a group can have more than a
marginal influence on market developments.

Following the extraordinary rise of free market prices from less
than 10 cents per pound at the time of the 1973 conference to a peak
of over 65 cents in November 1974 and their equally precipitous return
to the 1973 level in the second half of 1976, another United Nations
conference in Geneva in 1977 succeeded in negotiating a new International Sugar Agreement with economic provisions, which came into
force on 1 January 1978. Cuba's proposal of a price range of 15–25
cents per pound was whittled down in the negotiations to 11–21 cents.
At the time of writing (May 1978), the free market price has not yet
re-entered this range, the lower part of which is considered to reflect
present average costs of production of efficient producers. An early test
of the upper limit of the range appears unlikely at this time and, however much desired by sugar exporters, would not be in their long-term
interest. Another price boom would not only fuel the secular trend toward self-sufficiency among importing countries, but also stimulate
competition from a new source. In the last few years, an alternative
sweetener, high-fructose corn syrup, has begun to make inroads into the
markets for sugar, particularly in the United States and Japan. It is this
sort of structural change with which Cuban policy makers have yet to
come to terms.

References

Bernardo, Gerardo. 1963. La tercera zafra del pueblo. *Hoy Domingo* (Havana),
11 August.

Boorstein, Edward. 1968. *The Economic Transformation of Cuba*. New York
and London: Monthly Review Press.

Castro Ruz, Fidel. 1970a. Report on the sugar harvest. Speech, 20 May. In
Cuba in Revolution, Rolando E. Bonachea and Nelson P. Valdés, eds.,
1972. Garden City, N.Y.: Doubleday/Anchor Books, 261–304.

———. 1970b. Report on the Cuban economy. Speech, 26 July. In *Cuba in
Revolution*, Rolando E. Bonachea and Nelson P. Valdés, eds., 1972. Garden City, N.Y.: Doubleday/Anchor Books, 317–56.

Dorticós Torrado, Osvaldo. 1974. Speech to veterans of the sugar industry. 10
October. *ATAC* (Havana) 33 (4–6):15–21.

Hagelberg, G. B. 1974. *The Caribbean Sugar Industries: Constraints and Opportunities*. New Haven: Yale University, Antilles Research Program,
Occasional Papers, No. 3.

International Sugar Council, 1963. *The World Sugar Economy: Structure and Policies. Vol. II: The World Picture.* London.

International Sugar Council/Organization. 1956ff. *Sugar Yearbook.* London.

Matthews, Herbert L. 1969. *Fidel Castro.* New York: Simon and Schuster.

Vázquez, José. 1973a. Entrevista con Raúl León Torras. *ATAC* (Havana) 32 (2):4–14.

——. 1973b. Entrevista a Marcelo Fernández Font, Ministro de Comercio Exterior de Cuba. *ATAC* (Havana) 32(5/6):16–29.

——. 1974. Entrevista al Viceministro de Producción del Minaz, Luis de la Fe. *ATAC* (Havana) 33(1):15–21.

In addition, the author has relied on C. Czarnikow Ltd., *Sugar Review*, and various publications of the West German sugar statistical service F. O. Licht.

Cuba's Membership in the CMEA

EDWARD A. HEWETT

It is really quite inconvenient that Cuba has joined CMEA—the Council for Mutual Economic Assistance (also known as COMECON). CMEA specialists rarely talk to those scholars who are knowledgeable in Cuban affairs, don't for the most part read Spanish, and know little of the secondary literature about Cuba; and vice versa for Cuba specialists. Moreover, Cuba's 1972 decision to join CMEA would seem at first glance to set a new record for economic nonsense in CMEA affairs. Cuba—a small, underdeveloped island economy—suddenly announces it is joining a customs union of rich socialist countries one-fourth of the way around the globe. It is one thing to be a major recipient of generous Soviet aid in the face of a trade embargo by most of one's former trade partners; but quite another to join the CMEA and become involved in intricate designs for the division of labor, integration, plan coordination, and so on. Cuba has no common language and culture with the CMEA countries; the transportation costs are huge; and there is no genuine mutual appreciation of Marx and Lenin. The rational policy would most surely be to get all the aid and loans possible (if the price is right), trade only what is profitable, but try very hard to normalize trade relations with American countries, which for numerous reasons are, in the long run, much more logical trade partners.

Why then does Cuba appear to be following another path, one apparently against her long-term interests? There seem to be two possible explanations for this puzzle. The primarily political explanation is that Cuba had no choice in the matter: the Russians used the tremendous leverage of Cuba's accumulated debts with the U.S.S.R. to force Cuba into CMEA. This makes a good deal of sense from the Soviet point of view. They can boast that CMEA spans three continents: Asia, Europe, and America. In a more practical vein they can formally spread the cost of subsidizing Cuba among other CMEA member-states.

But the other possible explanation, which makes more sense from Cuba's point of view, is that there is no real puzzle. Perhaps there are very good economic reasons for Cuba to join CMEA, that is, the actual costs of membership may be far below the apparent ones, and the actual benefits may exceed the obvious ones.

My research reported in this paper tends to support parts of both explanations. The Soviets are obviously making a great deal of noise about Cuba's membership in CMEA and its significance for humankind; but Cuba's membership in CMEA seems to be a real bargain compared to the costs to all other members. The following section contains a brief discussion of the operation of CMEA, necessary to understand the special nature of Cuba's membership. In the next section Cuba's membership is discussed. A final section contains some speculative comments concerning the future of Cuba in CMEA.

The conclusions I reach in this paper are tentative, for several reasons. First, I read Russian, but not Spanish; therefore I relied primarily on Soviet sources. I was able, however, to use some Cuban sources through translations contained in the Joint Publications Research Service's Translations on Latin America. Secondly, I could find little information about the actual terms under which Cuba joined CMEA, yet it is in these details that the potential costs and benefits of membership are grounded. Thus, in many cases I must extrapolate from fragmentary information.

The Council for Mutual Economic Assistance

For present purposes it will suffice to outline CMEA activities in order to understand what type of organization Cuba has joined. More detailed accounts of CMEA are available elsewhere (Kaser 1967; Hewett 1974: chs. 1, 6).

CMEA was formally established in 1949 by Bulgaria, Czechoslovakia, Hungary, Poland, Romania, and the Soviet Union. East Germany and Albania joined later the same year; Albania withdrew and Mongolia joined in 1962; and Cuba joined in 1972. The official goals of CMEA were to encourage the development of mutual aid and trade among the socialist countries.[1] In fact it appears that Stalin forced the

founding of the organization for the quite different purpose of giving
a visible, socialist answer to the proposals for Marshall Plan aid which
had come to several socialist countries. Thus CMEA began its existence
as an act of defiance against Western policies and not as a positive action concerning socialist economic relations. Until the mid-1950s
CMEA did almost nothing as an organization; Stalin's last years, and
the political maneuvering in Moscow after his death, combined to im-
mobilize international relations among the socialist countries.

In the late 1950s CMEA became a more active international economic organization. In the CMEA sessions and committee meetings,
discussions and debates took place on the interrelated questions of plan
coordination, specialization (division of labor), and pricing. These are
difficult questions, particularly so because CMEA is the first economic
organization of its kind. It performs for socialist, centrally planned
economies the functions which a customs union performs for regulated
capitalist market economies by setting a constant bias in favor of inter-
member trade, by coordinating economic policies, and so on. But it
must do these things in a different way since these are centrally planned
economies; and there are no previous role models to follow. Since the
1950s there has emerged, from the many debates and several declara-
tions, something of a consensus of what these countries perceive to be
the role of an international economic organization of centrally planned
economies:

1. CMEA has no powers to command, that is, it is not a supranational
   planning organization. It is a forum for debate and discussion of
   issues relating to international trade and specialization among the
   socialist countries, but it can only recommend solutions.
2. Even if central planning is working as well as can be expected in
   individual CMEA countries, there are still substantial possibilities
   for increasing efficiency, hence economic growth, by specialization
   and trade among CMEA members. CMEA is an appropriate organization to seek out those possibilities and guide the member countries
   to bilateral and multilateral negotiations with the goal of exploiting
   the possibilities.
3. The mechanisms for encouraging specialization and trade must reflect the planning mechanisms within the countries; thus the focus
   of CMEA activities is increasingly on such projects as:
   (a) The coordination of medium-term plans, including estimates of
       future trade flows, commitments on capital flows among mem-
       bers, coordination of major investment projects, and coordina-
       tion of major economic policies which have significance outside
       individual member countries.

(b) Devising guidelines and supervising negotiations on specific decisions concerning specialization among countries. This is primarily handled through a set of standing commissions within CMEA concerned with specific industries, which make recommendations on such matters as which countries should specialize in producing various parts of the entire profile of computers in demand by all members of the CMEA community.

(c) Making recommendations on pricing for intramember trade, for the purpose of establishing fair terms of trade in the absence of active markets.

(d) Coordination of research and development activities within CMEA in order to minimize duplication of effort, enjoy economies of scale, and increase the rate of technical change in all countries.

(e) Joint prognosis of future events in order to coordinate projections, check for inconsistencies, and so on.

4. In addition, CMEA has attempted to decrease bureaucratic and physical impediments to trade, for example through the promulgation of standard contracts, through the attempt to coordinate rational use of excess railroad car capacity throughout the area, and through studies of containerization.

This is not an exhaustive list, but it covers the main principles which have evolved in CMEA's thirty years of existence. It should be emphasized that these principles have *evolved*. They have not been decided as matters of fundamental agreement among socialist countries; rather, they are the outcome of many sometimes fierce debates among warring factions over specific policy questions which had implications for general principles.

One strong faction which has lost many battles has been led by the Soviet Union. Throughout the last twenty-five years, and particularly the last twenty, the Soviets have lobbied more or less constantly for a stronger CMEA administration which would take on some functions typical of central planning bureaus in individual countries, particularly in the area of investment planning. The Romanians have led the opposition to these moves and seem to have successfully stymied them so far (Hewett 1974: ch. 1). At present CMEA is primarily a meeting-house and a facilitator, in a way a type of "confederacy" for the individual member countries.

There are two international organizations peripheral to CMEA which have somewhat more power and are of particular importance to Cuba's membership. The International Bank for Economic Cooperation (IBEC) was established in 1964 and acts as a settlements bank and source of short-term capital for trade among the CMEA countries. The unit of account is the transferable ruble (TR), which has a formal exchange rate equal to that of the Soviet ruble but which is actually a different currency in several respects. It is not, for example, represented by physical pieces of paper; essentially the TR is created by imbalances in trade among the member-countries. Also, the actual prices which are denominated in TRs are different from Soviet domestic prices; therefore the TR and the Soviet ruble have different real purchasing powers.

The main *de facto* function of the TR is to serve as an accounting device which registers intra-CMEA trade flows originally denominated in various currencies. The TR is not, however, a convertible currency; that is, it does not act as a store of value or medium of exchange. Theoretically a surplus in, say, Polish-Soviet trade can be used by Poland to finance imports from any other CMEA country; but actually that is not the case at all. Nonzero balances between two CMEA countries are usually removed in future years of trade between those two countries.

The International Investment Bank (IIB) is another important financial institution which links the CMEA countries but which is organizationally outside CMEA. The IIB was established in 1971 for the purpose of financing long-term capital flows among CMEA countries. It is financed out of contributions from individual CMEA countries (through 1974 a total of 368 billion TRs, 30 percent of which was in hard currencies) and through loans obtained from international financial markets. The IIB is charged with the task of financing long-term projects which employ advanced technology and intend the eventual production of goods to be supplied to several CMEA members. It is, in other words, the financial instrument of the CMEA countries' aspirations for long-term specialization and trade.

These institutions are designed to facilitate the expansion of trade and mutually coordinated investment among the CMEA countries. They are not part of CMEA but do have agreements with that organization and serve as extensions of CMEA. In addition, CMEA itself takes on part of the task of coordination by recommending forms of negotiation on trade agreements and actual procedures for pricing trade.

Intra-CMEA trade is primarily controlled by medium-term trade agreements (typically covering five years) and annual trade protocols which act to implement the agreements. Those agreements are the results of negotiations, typically at the ministerial level, and are usually implemented by individual foreign trade organizations in each of the

CMEA countries. The protocols are the most active controllers of trade; they specify in detail the quantities to be traded and the prices, thus the terms of trade.

Intra-CMEA trade prices have presented tremendous difficulties for the CMEA countries. Markets are inactive and therefore there is no mechanism which automatically generates pressures for uniform and meaningful prices. But uniform and meaningful prices are very important for intra-CMEA trade since the bilateral trade flows contain too many complicated commodities for direct barter agreements. The CMEA countries have chosen to generate their prices through a bargaining process in which the fundamental rule is supposed to be that prices in intra-CMEA trade will reflect world market prices for some past period. But in fact that is not what happens: machinery and equipment prices are relatively much higher in intra-CMEA trade, and primary product prices relatively lower, than on the world markets—an irony since it is primary products, not machinery and equipment, which are scarce on CMEA markets. Political problems have prevented the dramatic changes in prices necessary to bring them more nearly into line both with world market prices and with CMEA scarcities; hence there is a semi-barter negotiating process in which countries with scarce primary products for sale will generally sell them only to other CMEA countries which will offer in return other scarce primary products. The only exception to this rule appears to be Soviet trade with other CMEA members; the U.S.S.R. exports mostly relatively low-priced primary products to the CMEA countries in exchange for relatively high-priced machinery and equipment (Ausch 1972; Hewett 1974: ch. 3).

Cuba in CMEA: Economic Effects

The interesting question about Cuba's membership in CMEA is whether it will bring a net economic improvement or deterioration relative to the situation which would have obtained if Cuba had not joined. Of course it may be, as I mentioned earlier, that Cuba had no choice in the matter, and that possibility will be considered in more detail below; but here that consideration does not matter. The question now is whether or not, assuming Cuba had a genuine choice, it would have been better off not to join CMEA.

From the description of CMEA institutions in the last section, we can surmise the major changes in Cuba's economic relations that may result from its decision to join CMEA. However, before discussing those changes, it is necessary to outline the character of Cuban economic relations with the CMEA countries before 1972.

CUBA'S ECONOMIC RELATIONS WITH THE CMEA COUNTRIES BEFORE 1972

The most striking characteristic of the period from 1960 to 1972 was the overwhelming importance of the Soviet Union in Cuba's relations with the CMEA countries. The Soviet Union has consistently accounted for three-fourths, and usually more, of the CMEA countries' exports to Cuba. In the late 1960s, as Cuba's deficits with the Soviet Union grew large, the Soviet share in CMEA exports to Cuba rose to around 85 percent. Soviet imports from Cuba have typically ranged between 65 and 70 percent of all CMEA imports (VT, various issues). Before 1972 probably three-fourths of all aid from the CMEA countries to Cuba, in the form either of loans for specific projects or of accumulated deficits, came from the Soviet Union (Baklanoff 1971:369).

In many ways these numbers understate the importance of the Soviet Union to Cuba during this period; for it is probable that the Soviet Union alone made the difference between survival and extinction for the Cuban Revolution. This is most apparent in the interrelated areas of aid and trade, which are discussed in detail in the appendix, and will be only summarized here.

Total Soviet exports to Cuba during the 1960–72 period were worth 5,542.9 million rubles. The Cubans were able to pay with their own exports for 3,310.6 million rubles' worth of those Soviet goods, or 60 percent. Since Soviet-Cuban trade has always been conducted on the basis of some sort of clearing dollar rather than convertible currencies, the remainder of these Soviet exports, 2,232.3 million rubles, is in fact the true value of Soviet aid to Cuba. It represents the reported ruble value of goods shipped to Cuba for which Cuba was not forced to pay immediately either directly, in the form of goods, or indirectly, in goods exported to earn convertible currencies to use in payment for Soviet shipments.

Of that deficit, somewhat more than 479 million rubles, or 8.6 percent of the value of all Soviet exports to Cuba, was covered in formal development loans to Cuba. The remaining 1,753.3 million rubles, or 31.4 percent, the Cubans simply couldn't pay for; so the Soviets were forced to give what I would call "unplanned" loans. That means that of the total value of Soviet aid to Cuba during this period, only 21 percent represented loans formally granted.

The following illustrative calculation gives some idea of the importance of total Soviet aid to the Cubans. During 1968–69 total Cuban imports were about 16 percent of what they call Gross Social Product, which is close to the U.N. concept of Gross Domestic Product (GDP) (EIU, 1975 *Annual Supplement*, 4 and 13). About 60 percent of those imports were from the U.S.S.R. These numbers indicate the general orders of magnitude during the entire period under discussion. Since in the 1960–72 period about 40 percent of Cuban imports from the Soviet Union came in the form of loans, about one-fourth of all Cuban imports during these thirteen years came on loan from the Soviet Union. That means that, on average, the Soviets loaned the Cubans about 4 percent of their GDP every year during this period.

But the Soviet contribution was even more important than that. The commodities the Soviets loaned, particularly in the unplanned loans, were intermediate commodities crucial to Cuba's continued production of much of its GDP. The planned loans were primarily granted to finance machinery and equipment necessary for the growth of GDP; the unplanned loans financed mostly intermediate goods and primary products necessary to the production of current GDP. For example, from the very first in 1960 the Soviets supplied the Cubans' needs in petroleum and petroleum products after the U.S. cut off exports to Cuba (Bondarchuk 1973:2). Around 1970 Soviet exports of petroleum and petroleum products to Cuba were about 10 percent of the value of all Soviet exports; by 1972–73 the proportion was up to over 15 percent.

Another important example, which actually comes under the heading of machinery and equipment in the trade data, is spare parts for old American equipment. Since the early 1960s the Soviets have been specially machining spare parts for Cuba's old American equipment, primarily in the nickel, petroleum, sugar, and cement industries (Vladimirskii 1972:15). For example, in 1967 Cuba submitted orders to the Soviets for spare parts for the nickel industry for the period 1969–72. The average annual shipments were anticipated to be worth about 2.8 million dollars a year during those four years (Bekarevich and Kukharev 1973:35).

What these two examples show—and others could be drawn easily —is that the particular 4 percent of Cuban GDP which the Soviets loaned every year was composed of goods of considerable importance to the production of the other 96 percent of GDP.

One of the real problems in assessing the true importance of all of these numbers involves export and import prices. After all, the deficit in Cuba's trade with the Soviet Union could easily be doubled or wiped out simply by changing the prices of Soviet shipments to Cuba, or of Cuban shipments to the Soviet Union. Since this is a bilateral trade flow with few desirable alternative markets for the Cubans and special reasons for Soviet interest, there is really no market working to generate prices close to world market prices.

In fact, not surprisingly, there is little public information about Cuban-Soviet foreign trade prices in this period.[2] The trade agreements stipulated that prices would be based on those of basic world markets.[3] The actual pricing arrangements, however, were worked out in detailed protocols to the agreements themselves, and these have not been published.[4]

The fact that world market prices (WMPs) were supposedly the base for pricing in Cuban-Soviet trade during this period is hardly sufficient evidence to conclude that the real prices had anything to do with WMPs. A similar clause in some form has been in all intra-CMEA trade agreements since the late 1940s, yet, as mentioned above, there is substantial evidence that actual intra-CMEA trade prices deviate greatly and systematically from WMPs. On the other hand, there is evidence of a more circumstantial nature which would tend to support the idea that Cuban-Soviet prices did not deviate substantially from WMPs, or that when they did, it was to Cuba's advantage.

The U.S.S.R. is, after all, in a rather weak position in Latin America. As the Soviets themselves claim, competition with Western firms is stiff, and they (the Soviets) are predominant in no Latin American markets outside Cuba (Gladkov 1972). This means two things. First, Soviet export and import prices with Latin America probably lie close to WMPs in that area, if not below them for exports and above them for imports. Competition plus some bias against the Soviets would suggest as much. For that reason alone one would suspect that the Soviets would have a hard time charging Cuba more than, or paying it less than, the prices typical in Latin American foreign trade. Also, Cuba is for the Soviets a showcase in Latin America and therefore one would expect Cuban terms of trade with the Soviet Union to be better than those for Latin America overall. Consequently, it seems likely that the Soviets traded with Cuba at prices which—from the Cubans' point of view—were as good as, or better than, those they would have faced on world markets. On at least one price—sugar—we know Cuba did better than it could have on world markets. The same reasons would suggest that WMPs were also used in East European–Cuban trade.

All of this means that if we were to reprice the Cuban-Soviet deficit in terms of WMPs, rather than using official exchange rates (which assume that all ruble prices are related to WMPs by the single, official exchange rate), then the deficit would probably be about the same size; if not—if the Soviets were charging prices for exports below

WMPs and systematically paying prices above WMPs for imports from Cuba—the deficit would be even larger.

Another point to keep in mind about the deficit is that not all of it is really development aid in the true sense; some if it was necessary to cover the costs imposed by the U.S. blockade. There were the direct costs of switching from primarily U.S. equipment to Soviet equipment. (For example, U.S. equipment operates on 60 hertz, Soviet equipment on 50 hertz.) There were also the substantial costs which accrue because the major trade partner is thousands of miles away: a much larger merchant marine; a better material-technical supply system; the need for larger stocks, thus new storage facilities; construction of newer and better ports; and so on (Bondarchuk 1973:5). Finally, there were defense-related costs which diverted funds that otherwise could have been invested. All of these costs are previews to the costs which will accrue to Cuba if it continues its membership in CMEA along with the trade diversion that implies. The difference between these costs and those involved in future years of integration with CMEA is that the former were unavoidable. The U.S. embargo and the Soviet Union's willingness to aid Cuba in nullifying its influence left no choice then.

Eastern Europe played a much different and less significant role than the Soviets during the period before 1972. In the early 1960s most East European countries followed the Soviet lead and offered development loans worth several hundred million rubles, of which the largest loans came from East Germany and Czechoslovakia (Baklanoff 1971: 269). The magnitude of this effort was quite small in proportion to the Soviet effort, and by the late 1960s the East Europeans were giving no substantial loans to Cuba. More importantly, there is no evidence that Eastern Europe was at all inclined to give out unplanned loans. Cuban–East European trade is much more like normal trade among states involved in bilateral trade agreements: over time it is for the most part balanced.

CUBA IN THE CMEA

Given the foregoing description of CMEA institutions and the reality of the 1960–72 relationship between Cuba and CMEA, especially between Cuba and the Soviet Union, it is very hard at first glance to see why Cuba would voluntarily decide to join CEMA. Cuba has enjoyed a very rich benefactor in the Soviet Union; its relations with the other CMEA countries have not been unusual, but that matters little: one rich benefactor is enough. Joining CMEA could hardly give Cuba a better deal with the Soviet Union or with the East European countries;

thus the net benefits from such a move appear slim indeed. On the other hand, it seems that potentially important costs would result from such a move.

The first and by far most important cost for Cuba would be changes in its terms of trade with the CMEA countries. If indeed up to 1972 Cuba's trade with the CMEA countries was valued at WMPs and if in joining CMEA it was forced to accept CMEA prices, substantial loss for Cuba could result. As mentioned earlier, CMEA prices significantly differ from WMPs, and in a particular way: machinery prices are relatively much higher than WMPs, while primary product prices are relatively lower. Almost all Cuba's exports are primary products, and a substantial portion of its imports are machinery and equipment. Hence Cuba's terms of trade with CMEA would probably fall somewhat, although it is almost impossible to estimate how much.

There could be substantial problems, too, in adopting the transferable ruble (TR), and in particular in joining the two banking systems discussed earlier, the International Bank for Economic Cooperation (IBEC) and the International Investment Bank (IIB). Consider, for example, the IIB. The IIB had a statutory capital (i.e., the amount of money capital which it could raise from its members in the form of contributions) of 1,052,600,000 TRs in 1973. The actual amount paid into the capital in 1973 was 367 million TRs: that is, the members had not yet subscribed the entire capital. The contributions must be 30 percent in hard currencies and the remainder in TRs. The hard currencies have to be actual payments of currency to the IIB; the TRs, since there is no actual currency of that sort, are generally created through surpluses generated by individual countries in their trade with other CMEA members. If Cuba joined IIB, I estimate that the statutory capital would rise to 1,078,840,000. That is, Cuba's full contribution to statutory capital would be 26.24 million TRs.[5] Upon entry Cuba would have to subscribe only about one-third of its full statutory capital quota, as the other members have, which would be a little under 9 million TRs. Thirty percent of that, or about 2.7 million TRs, would have to be in convertible currency.

Now, of course, the problem with Cuba's joining the IIB—and an identical problem would arise for the IBEC—is that it has no surplus with the CMEA countries and thus could not subscribe even the 9 million TRs without another Soviet loan. The 2.7 million TRs in convertible currency would be impossible unless the Soviets would loan Cuba the money. Membership in these two banks is not required of CMEA members; but such membership would be hard to avoid, particularly in the IBEC, since all CMEA payments are denominated in TRs and go through that bank.

There is another potential cost involved in Cuba's membership in CMEA which is less tangible, yet nevertheless potentially serious. CMEA is preoccupied now with pursuing integration and specialization and with achieving larger gains from trade, hence more rapid growth. This means that the predominant emphasis is on static comparative advantage—on the factor endowments and comparative advantages which exist at present within CMEA. Romania, which has more than twice the per capita GNP of Cuba and is much more developed, has fought this orientation for years. For countries at Romania's level of development (and this would apply even more to Cuba), the emphasis on static gains from trade within CMEA tends to assign them the long-term production of simple manufactured goods, primary products, fruits, and so on. Romania has complained repeatedly that this smacks of capitalist trade patterns, so frequently condemned by socialist polemicists as exploitative of poorer countries.

CMEA countries frequently reiterate their commitment to equalizing the levels of development of all member countries; and growth rates show that this is happening. But the policy and the fact may not be connected. More important, there is no sign that in decisions on investment allocations and specialization of tasks the CMEA countries are willing to give their less developed members the chance to change their comparative advantages in favor of more sophisticated commodities. To the extent this is a valid observation, Cuba was ill-advised to join CMEA because of the impact that move might have on the future structure of Cuba's economic system. There is, for example, a real danger that if Cuba remains in CMEA it will become the major supplier of sugar and nickel, but not much else. How much different is that scenario from the one which would have been obtained in the absence of the Revolution?

In sum, to this point in the discussion it appears that the potential benefits to Cuba from its membership in CMEA are very few, and the potential costs are significant; there seems to be no support in the economics of the situation for Cuba's decision to join. However, there are some interesting, although quite fragmentary, bits of information which suggest that Cuba has been allowed to enter CMEA under very special conditions which eliminate many of the potential costs listed above.

For example, Cuba did join the IIB and IBEC in 1974 (Konstantinov 1975:82). But the 1974 year-end balance sheets for both banks show no new contributions to capital in 1974.[6] In fact, the statutory capital for IBEC didn't even change. That of the IIB did change, by 15.7 million TRs. That might be the Cuban contribution; but if it is, then it is probably just the TR portion (70 percent of the total). If that is the case, then the estimate given above for Cuba's share of an increased IIB capital is too high. Finally, if 15.7 million TRs represent the total change in statutory capital due to Cuba's entry, and not just the nonconvertible portion, then Cuba received a very good deal indeed.[7]

Despite Cuba's lack of any contribution to the banks, it is evidently able to avail itself fully of their credit services. For example, Cuba is slated to receive a loan from the IIB for the construction of the Victor de Khitron citrus plant (EG, 1975, no. 20 [May], p. 21; no. 21 [May], p. 20). Also, the IBEC is evidently granting Cuba short-term credits at interest rates ranging from 0.5 to 2.5 percent, which are quite favorable in comparison with rates of 2–5 percent charged other members (Konstantinov 1975:85).[8]

There is no direct evidence on what changes have occurred in Cuba's terms of trade with CMEA since 1972. But one interesting fact is that when Cuba signed a trade agreement with Hungary in 1973, the year after it joined CMEA, the agreement was denominated in clearing pesos, not TRs (Bazsó 1975). That is a change from the previous practice in Hungarian-Cuban trade of using clearing dollars, but it is not a change to the practice typical in intra-CMEA trade of denominating trade in TRs. What that suggests is that at least in Cuban-Hungarian trade there has been no move into conformity with CMEA prices.

One doubts, in fact, that any CMEA country will force major terms-of-trade losses on Cuba now. That would simply increase Cuba's trade deficit since whatever prices the CMEA countries want to use, Cuba's real export possibilities will be just the same in the short run. Also, it is quite common practice in CMEA to allow actual prices in trade to deviate substantially from the prices promised in trade agreements, since to enforce the established prices would mean pressing heavy losses on a few CMEA members. This has been particularly true in Soviet–East European trade, and will probably hold for a while in CMEA-Cuban trade.

It is too early to assess the impact of the third potential cost mentioned in Cuba's joining CMEA: that of perpetuating the present structure of Cuban exports. It was most likely this very fear that placed on the agenda of the Cuban-Soviet 1973–75 Trade and Cooperation Agreement negotiations the topic of expanding the range of goods produced in Cuba (Kukharev 1973:14). The outcome of this matter will depend on the outcome of many individual decisions which are still in the future. Limitations on Cuba's economic diversity, however, could be the most formidable cost which Cuba has to bear. The particular combination of countries now represented by CMEA is unparalleled in other customs unions; the others all tend to have predominantly rich or poor members and not mixtures of the two, because the rich and poor countries have dramatically different interests and needs. It remains to be seen whether Cuba will be able to satisfy its special interests and needs in CMEA, or whether the CMEA countries will use Cuba to satisfy theirs.

The economic costs, then, of Cuba's membership in CMEA are probably not as high as they might have been. The very sketchy information available at present suggests that Cuba is a very special member of CMEA, special in such a way that the costs of membership are quite low.

The Soviet Union seems to have moved in several ways to sweeten the benefits of membership for Cuba, in addition to the special concessions mentioned above. In December 1972, less than six months after Cuba's formal accession, the Soviets granted Cuba a new loan of 300 million rubles for technical aid during 1973–75. More important, as mentioned earlier, it postponed repayment of the enormous deficit accumulated through December 1972 not covered under formal agreements. There are no more interest charges; repayment begins in 1986 and is spread over twenty-five years. There was also agreement on a substantially higher sugar price (EIU, 1973, no. 1, p. 4). The timing of these changes, and of Castro's visit to the U.S.S.R. and Eastern Europe, would suggest that they were almost a payment for entering the CMEA.

After Cuba's entry there was also the implied commitment that all CMEA countries would participate in major investments to help Cuba better exploit its huge nickel deposits. That agreement was subsequently formalized and signed by all CMEA members in July 1975 (EG, 1975, no. 27 [July], p. 3).

Conclusion

Why did the Cubans join CMEA? Probably because the Soviets wanted them to. It is a logical step in what is beginning to look like strong Soviet pressure for the Cubans to institutionalize the role of the Communist Party in Cuban society and to institutionalize Cuba's relations with the other socialist countries. The realization of those goals has substantial political payoffs for the Soviet Union, which is anxious to increase its influence in Latin America. Nicholas Faddev, the secretary of CMEA, commented on Cuba's accession to the organization as follows:

The entry of Cuba into CMEA has great political significance. It is the first country on the American continent which has become a member of an international organization unifying socialist countries. Now there are members from all three continents in CMEA: Europe, Asia, and America. The entry of Cuba is testimony of the generality of interests of socialist countries, irrespective of what part of the world they are in. [Faddev 1974:52]

Another possible Soviet motive may have been to spread the costs of subsidizing Cuba's further development among CMEA members. That, in effect, is what happens when the IIB rather than the Soviet Union finances projects, or when the IBEC rather than the Soviet Union finances deficits, or when all CMEA members, rather than the Soviet Union alone, agree to build nickel plants in Cuba.

Finally, the Soviets may have seen in CMEA membership an institutionalized vehicle for changing Cuba's economic and political system into the more rigid, familiar, East European mode. Cuba has experimented with various types of planning techniques with no notable successes; one common characteristic of all the experiments is that they have never really sought to institutionalize the full-blown, realistic, macro planning system typical of Eastern Europe—the kind of system that balances all major commodities in annual plans, medium-term plans, and so on (Mesa-Lago and Zephirin 1971). It would appear that around 1970 the Soviets began to put increasing pressure on the Cubans to move in the direction of more orthodox planning methods.

This was probably the purpose of the Soviet-Cuban Commission on Economic and Scientific-Technical Cooperation, established in 1970 for the purpose of working out proposals for cooperation between planning organs, ministries, and departments (Bekarevich and Kukharev 1973:10). In discussing the commission, one Soviet author notes that a past problem in dealing with Cuba had been inadequate plan coordination, since agreements were signed on a year-by-year basis; the commission was cited as a step towards improvement (Bondarchuk 1973:6). The commission quite obviously was well suited as a vehicle for Soviet pressure towards more comprehensive and detailed plans; that is, without detailed plans there would be no long-term cooperation. One suspects that Cuba resisted the pressure as best it could. No doubt there were pressures within Cuba towards improved planning in the aftermath of the 1970 harvest problems; but one doubts that there was strong pressure for a Soviet-type planning mechanism. One small piece of evidence of such resistance comes from an interview Deputy Prime Minister Carlos Rafael Rodríguez granted directly after the first

meeting of the commission in December 1971. He had noted to his interviewer that a big advantage of the commission was the institutionalization of Soviet-Cuban cooperation and provision of a basis for the
realization of cooperative projects. The interviewer asked him if that
would not require planning on the part of Cuba, and his answer was,
"Most certainly." Rodríguez cited the example of French-Soviet cooperation—the implication being that if the Soviets could cooperate so
effectively with an "indicatively" planned system without having a
major impact on the system, they could do so with Cuba (Rodríguez
1971:53).

Later on in the interview Rodríguez noted that a full program of
Soviet-Cuban cooperation had been in the early discussion stage several
years earlier, but it might take more than a decade to implement because it was intertwined with the principle of introducing medium-
and long-term plans into the Cuban economic system (p. 57).

The entry into CMEA would, therefore, seem a logical extension
of Soviet pressure for system change in Cuba. The numerous standing
commissions involved in cooperation in various industries, the plan
coordination sessions, the exchanges of delegations on planning, and
so on, would all serve to create pressures for Cuba to move towards a
system more similar to that prevalent in the CMEA countries. After
all, it is quite difficult to participate in sessions for coordinating five-
year plans if one does not have a plan! Just after Cuba's entry into
CMEA, two Soviet authors published an article in the party journal
Kommunist; the main point of it was that Cuba was finally coming to
realize the necessity for greater reliance on material incentives and on
complete plans. They pictured Cuba as finally setting up planning
on a "more realistic, scientifically based foundation with the utilization
of the multi-faceted experience of the countries of socialism" (Gorbachev and Darynsenkov 1973:89).

That the Soviets would have had the leverage to force Cuba into
CMEA should be quite evident by now. The enormous debt Cuba had
accumulated with the Soviet Union, equal to more than several years'
worth of her total exports to the world, was sufficient for the Soviets
to exert considerable influence on most major aspects of Cuba's economic system and on Cuba's economic policy.

But the puzzling question, then, is why the Soviets, and through
them CMEA, gave such special consideration to Cuba for its joining
CMEA? The obvious answer—which must contain some part of the
truth—is that the Soviets could put any price they wanted on Cuba's
entry into CMEA, but if it were greater than zero they would have had
to loan Cuba the money to join.

Some of the truth may also lie in a not-so-obvious answer. Cuba is a very unusual country in CMEA in several ways. First, as pointed out earlier, it is in Latin America, an area where Soviet foreign policy has enjoyed no great success. Thus, Cuba is a showcase, it knows it, and it may have exploited that fact in negotiations with the Soviets as it has done in the past (Gonzalez 1971). Rodríguez noted in an interview for a Soviet publication that other Third World countries were watching Cuba and would turn to Cuba to find out what they could expect from membership in CMEA (Rodríguez 1975:34). One can imagine in the negotiating sessions the Cubans constantly pointing to the fact that they were a test case for Latin America, a bellwether for the future development of CMEA relations with that part of the world.

Finally, there must be some negotiating power which accrues to the Cubans because they are a regime with foundations in their own revolution. Castro is a successful revolutionary; his government is the result of a full-scale revolution. In that, he is unique among all the CMEA countries save the Soviet Union; it gives him something the East European countries have much less of—a source of legitimacy outside his ties with the Soviet Union.

For all of these reasons—Soviet desires and power, and Cuban desires and power—the membership of Cuba in the CMEA seems on further study to make much more sense than it does on first glance. The evidence is not all in, either because the information is not published (or is published in languages to which I do not have access), or because the full effects of Cuba's membership in CMEA have not had time to work themselves out. But it appears at this point that Cuba joined CMEA under growing pressure from the Soviet Union; the *de facto* terms of membership were such as to minimize the costs of such a move; and the actual benefits are a continuation of the special relationship with the U.S.S.R. (now somewhat diverted through CMEA financial institutions).

In the long term, more substantial impacts will show up. The economic system may continue to change substantially; the structure of Cuban industry and Cuban exports might not change, but the volume of production and exports could grow tremendously. The most interesting unknown in the long-term relationship is the U.S. restrictions on trade with Cuba. When those are lifted, as they probably will be within a few years, there will be tremendous pressures for Cuba to redirect a substantial portion of its trade back to the U.S. The Soviets may already have this in mind, and in fact this is one other possible motive for their bringing Cuba into CMEA. But the Cubans must also be thinking of it, and it may be that their short-term policy is to join CMEA, continue to enjoy the large credits and deficits, and bide their time until the U.S. moves to resume trade. Of course, for several reasons the Soviet share of Cuban trade will not again reach the low level of the 1950s for a very long time; the Cubans owe the U.S.S.R. a great deal of money and one doubts that they would try to default on Soviet loans; and the Soviets have been good trade partners. But when the United States, ninety miles from Cuba with high demands for sugar and nickel, decides to resume trade with Cuba, inevitably there will be a major shift in Cuba's trade. The degree of that shift depends in part on what commitments Cuba makes between now and then.

Appendix: Soviet Loans to Cuba, 1960–72

The Soviets have two ways of giving aid to Cuba: through formal agreements which specify in some detail the projects involved, repayment periods, and so on; and by allowing deficits to accumulate. This latter method is very easy in the Soviet-Cuban case since trade is bilateral with an automatic swing credit in each recent year of 30 million rubles. When either side goes above that amount in deficit, the difference is subject to a 2 percent per annum interest charge. Consequently, each year when Cuba accumulates more than a 30-million-ruble deficit,[9] the Soviets automatically begin loaning Cuba rubles at 2 percent per annum (which, by the way, is 0.5 percent cheaper than the rate specified by the formal trade agreements). In this appendix, I will attempt to estimate Cuba's debt to the Soviet Union for the period 1960–72, as accumulated through these two mechanisms and through the interest due.

The major aid agreements between 1960 and 1972 are listed below according to the date the agreement was signed, the fundamental purposes of the loans, and the estimated amount (in current rubles).[10]

1. February 13, 1960. Ninety-million-ruble credit (denominated in dollars) for the construction of various enterprises in Cuba during 1961–65, the specific enterprises to be determined at a later date. The interest rate on the unpaid balance is 2.5 percent and repayment is to be in twelve equal annual installments, the payment commencing one year after the delivery of the equipment for every enterprise listed in the agreement, or after the completion of every task. The interest rate is charged on each part of the credit as it is used; and interest payments are due in the first quarter of the year following the year to which they apply. Repayment is to be in the form of sugar and other traditional Cuban exports.

In a subsequent agreement signed November 16, 1960, it was announced that this first loan would be used for geological exploration and expansion or construction of plants in the metallurgical, power generation, and petroleum industries.

2. June 1, 1961. Loan for the expansion of nickel and cobalt plants. Repayment for current expenses associated with the project and for machinery and equipment is to be made with nickel shipments. For machinery and equipment, repayment starts the year the equipment is delivered and must be completed within five years, with an interest rate on the unpaid balance of 2.5 percent. There is no statement of the actual value of this loan; Baklanoff estimates (1971:269) that its value is $100 million, i.e., 90 million rubles.

3. May 8, 1962. Loan for the development of the Cuban chemical industry. Repayment is with Cuban export goods; payments can be delayed up to five years; and there is a 2.5 percent annual interest charge on the unpaid balance. No indication is given of the value of this loan; Baklanoff estimates its value at $100 million, i.e., 90 million rubles (p. 269).[11]

4. January 11, 1963. Fourteen-million-ruble credit for delivery of machinery and equipment in 1963 connected with work on the irrigation and drainage of land. Repayment is according to the February 1960 agreement.

5. March 16, 1964. Fourteen-million-ruble credit for importation of machinery and equipment in 1964–65 for the same purposes as in the 1963 agreement. Repayment provisions are the same as in the 1960 and 1963 agreements.

6. September 6, 1964. Seventy-million-ruble credit for the reconstruction of the sugar industry, twelve years at 2.5 percent per annum. Repayment terms are the same as for the February 1960 credit. An additional 50-million-ruble credit was granted to finance purchase of transport equipment necessary in the rebuilding process. Repayments of that credit are to be over five years after the date of delivery, with an interest charge of 2.5 percent on the unpaid balance.

7. March 20, 1965. Twelve-million-ruble credit for materials and equipment necessary in geological exploration. Repayment terms as in the February 1960 agreement.

8. March 17, 1966. Two-million-ruble credit for equipment and other expenses associated with further work on irrigation and drainage. The actual value of the agreement is 4 million rubles, but 2 million is to be paid for through left-over funds in the 1963 and 1964 loans. The additional 2 million was added to the 1964 loan, making the total value of that loan 16 million rubles. Repayment of the addi-

tional 2 million rubles is to be at the same terms as for the 1963 and 1964 loans.

9. May 7, 1967. Thirty-million-ruble credit for importing equipment and for a second phase of the reconstruction of the sugar industry. This was actually added to the 1965 credit to make the total value of the twelve-year portion of that credit 100 million rubles. Repayment is, presumably, according to the 1965 agreement (this is implied but not made explicit).

10. January 15, 1968. Unspecified loan commitment by the Soviets to assist Cuba in the construction of electric transmission lines from Santiago de Cuba to Nuevitas. Part of the cost of this project is to be covered with an unused balance from the February 1960 agreement. The remainder is to be repaid over a five-year period with an interest rate of 2.5 percent on the unpaid balance.

11. January 7, 1969. Credit of unspecified amount to assist Cuba in reconstruction of its television broadcasting network. Repayment is over eight years with 2.5 percent interest on the unpaid balance.

12. January 8, 1970. Seven-million-ruble loan for construction of a relay station by mid-1972 capable of relaying telephone, telegraph, and television signals from Moscow to Havana with the assistance of satellites. Repayment is over twelve years with 2.5 percent interest on the unpaid balance.

13. March 13, 1970. Ten-million-ruble loan for technical assistance in geological work during 1971–72. Repayment according to February 1960 terms.

14. February 18, 1972. Loan for expansion of thermoelectric transmission lines. No other information.

15. February 22, 1972. Credit to Cuba. No other information.

16. December 23, 1972. Credit to Cuba allows it to defer payment on all credits issued to cover deficits through December 31, 1972; payments to start in 1986 and to span twenty-five years.[12]

These are all the credits reported in Bekarevich and Kukharev's work (1973). The numbers through 1969 agree with Baklanoff's (1971) in the main, although they differ in some details. Baklanoff does not claim to be exhaustive, so it is no matter that he left out the relatively minor credits numbered 4, 5, 8, 10, and 11. However, he does list the 1964 and 1967 credits for modernization of the sugar industry as one 100-million-ruble credit in 1964. Also, he does not mention the 50-million-ruble medium-term credit involved in the 1965 package on the sugar industry. He also seems to have missed the fact that the 1961 and 1962 credits were medium-term only.

The Bekarevich and Kukharev data seem to be the most complete available through the end of 1971, that is, up to the eve of Cuba's accession to CMEA. In total, over that period the Soviets awarded Cuba 479 million rubles in development loans, of which 230 million rubles were medium-term, five-year loans. The actual amount was somewhat higher than this since the value of several loans is not given in the agreements.

We can now compare these formal loan commitments with the actual deficit which obtained in Cuba's trade with the Soviet Union; it is that deficit which reflects the actual value of Soviet loans to Cuba since the deficit represents the value of goods which the Soviets shipped but for which the Cubans have not yet paid. Our data on loan agreements go through 1970; therefore, we will look at the deficit through the end of 1972, assuming that the actual purchases lagged by several years.

Between 1960 and 1972, the Soviet Union exported to Cuba 5,542.9 million rubles' worth of commodities; during that same period it imported 3,310.6 million rubles' worth of commodities. The difference, 2,232.3 million rubles, represents the value of Soviet goods loaned to Cuba during this period. We have found that 479 million rubles of that amount (and probably somewhat more) were covered by formal agreements; thus, the remaining 1,753.3 million rubles represent what I have called unplanned loans. No agreement was signed, other than the payments agreement, according to which these commitments become loans with a 2 percent interest rate.

The interest charges, of course, must be added in to obtain the full amount of Cuba's indebtedness to the Soviets by the end of 1972. That is difficult to do with any precision for several reasons. There is no indication, for example, of whether the medium-term loans in 1961 were paid off with Cuba's exports in subsequent years, in which case there would simply be a larger deficit in current payments and the loan would shift to a 2.0 percent debt. That would bring a different and somewhat smaller level of indebtedness than if the loans were treated as unpayable and simply extended at 2.5 percent on the whole balance. Furthermore, it is not clear, for many of the loans, when the Cubans actually had to begin repayment. This has an effect both on the interest rate and on the determination of the outstanding principal. While these problems prevent precise figures for Cuba's total indebtedness, they are sufficiently minor that we can make some reasonable assumptions and come up with a number which is probably fairly close to the correct one.

Let us assume that Cuba has defaulted on all loans, and that the Soviets have kept the interest charges up at 2.5 percent per year. Deficits not covered in the loans, for the period 1960–65, are subject to a 2.5 percent interest rate; after 1965 the interest rate is 2 percent.[13]

Table 1 / Soviet Loans to Cuba: Estimated Drawdowns
and Deficits by Year

	Drawdown*	Deficit (−)	Difference
1960	18	26.2	44.2
1961	36	22.4	58.4
1962	54	−119.5	−65.5
1963	68	−211.8	−143.8
1964	61	−70.2	−9.2
1965	79	−29.9	49.1
1966	44	−174.6	−130.6
1967	39	−171.2	−132.2
1968	39	−311.8	−272.8
1969	24	−353.1	−329.1
1970	17	−115.0	−98.0
1971	0	−313.1	−313.1
1972	0	−410.7	−410.7
Total	479	−2,232.3	−1,753.3

*All figures are in millions of rubles.

Source: VT, various issues.

Table 1 shows the distribution of drawdowns I have assumed (based
on my reading of the agreements), and I have decreased the yearly deficits by those amounts. These are extremely subjective guesses at drawdowns and almost certainly they are not correct; but they are probably
close enough; and in any event, errors are not as serious with a 2 percent interest rate as with a 9 percent interest rate.

Under the assumptions listed above, the interest owed by Cuba on
31 December 1972 on the principal of 2,232.3 million rubles comes out
to 96.62 million rubles on the formal development loans and 99.34
million rubles on the deficits, thus a total of 195.96 million rubles.
Despite the fact that the preponderance of the debt originates in the
unplanned deficits, the interest due on those is about the same as the
interest on the formal loans because of the somewhat lower interest
rate and the fact that the deficits did not begin to accumulate seriously
until the latter half of the 1960s.

The actual figure for interest plus principal is surely somewhat
different, for reasons already mentioned. We do not know the value of
all the loans, so the estimated principal is on the low side. We do not
know how unpaid loans are handled, and that could make a difference
in how much of the indebtedness was at 2 percent and not 2.5 percent

interest. The drawdown estimates are only illustrative and are not even a serious attempt to get at actual drawdowns, something which could be done, say, by looking carefully at various categories of Soviet machinery exports over this period. Finally, we do not know if or when the Soviets cancelled some interest due, with the exception of the December 1972 postponement of all payments due on the deficit. This also cancelled all future interest accrual on that part of the debt; but it isn't clear whether it cancelled the interest which accrued through December 1972.

Notes

1. See the communiqué announcing the establishment of CMEA, "K sozdaniiu Soveta Ekonomicheskoi Vzaimopomoshchi" ("Towards the Creation of the Council for Mutual Economic Assistance") in Tokareva 1972:121–22.

2. This secrecy is not, by the way, any indication that the actual prices favor the Soviets. It is quite clear, for example, in intra-CMEA trade where pricing details are also secret that it is the East Europeans and not the Soviets who benefit from the way actual prices are set (Hewett 1974: chs. 2–3).

3. See, for example, the 1965–70 trade agreement, article 7, for typical wording (Bekarevich and Kukharev 1973:226).

4. Vladimirskii mentions that there was a pricing protocol signed for the 1965–70 trade agreement (1972:15). But the most complete listing of agreements with which I am familiar (Bekarevich and Kukharev 1973) does not publish the protocol.

5. Since it is not quite clear how Cuba's joining the IIB would affect the statutory capital, the contribution required of Cuba is an estimate. The basic technique, as specified in the original agreement (Tokareva 1972: 257), is to compute each member-country's exports to all CMEA countries, compute the shares, and use those as each country's share of the total statutory capital. When new countries come in, the question is whether the statutory capital will remain at the same amount with a simple reallocation of the shares, or whether all the old countries' contributions will remain the same while the amount of the statutory capital is increased for the new country. In the case of Romania, which came in after the original agreement was signed, the statutory capital was increased from the 1 billion TRs originally agreed upon by the six charter members to 1,052,600,000 TRs. I have seen no published account of how the Romanian contribution was computed, but I have apparently succeeded in reconstructing it. Evidently, the ratio was established between Romania's exports to CMEA in 1970 and any other IIB member's exports to CMEA in 1970, and that ratio was multiplied by the IIB member's share to find Romania's share of the original billion. Using that technique, I estimate that Romania's entry

should have increased the statutory capital by 52.69 million TRs; in fact, it increased it by 52.60 million TRs, which seems acceptably close. If CMEA follows the same policy with Cuba, then I estimate the increase in statutory capital at 26.24 million TRs (based on 1973 trade data). (All data for these estimates are from CMEA 1971 and 1974.)

6. The IBEC balance sheets for 1973 and 1974 were published in EG in May 1975 (no. 21, p. 20), as were the IIB balance sheets (no. 20, p. 21).

7. The IIB balance sheet does show a slight change in the amount of actual capital paid in, an increase of 1.420 million TRs. I am assuming that that is probably either interest or principal payments on earlier loans.

8. Mongolia also receives special interest rates from the IBEC ranging from 0.5 to 1 percent.

9. See, for example, article 3 of the 1965–70 Payments Agreement between the Soviet Union and Cuba, which is published in Bekarevich and Kukharev 1973:228–31.

10. Unless otherwise stated, the information is from Bekarevich and Kukharev 1973, which contains copies of the loan agreements.

11. I have no idea what Baklanoff's sources are in these two cases and therefore cannot judge how reliable his estimates might be. I have found in going through the actual agreements that his sources are apparently mistaken on several points, which I indicate below.

12. Bondarchuk (1973:6) simply mentions December 1972. Bekarevich and Kukharev (1973) simply state that a credit agreement was signed on this date, and they list no other in December 1972.

13. The relevant articles in the payments agreements are in Bekarevich and Kukharev 1973:194, 229. In the calculations following, I have ignored the swing credits of 9 million rubles through 1965 and 27 million rubles thereafter, since presumably those refer to the status of loaned capital at the end of the period along with the remainder of the deficit.

References

Abbreviations used: JPRS—Joint Publications Research Service; MCUSGP—Monthly Catalogue of U.S. Government Publications.

Ausch, Sandor. 1972. *Theory and Practice of CMEA Cooperation*. Budapest: Akadémiai Kiadó.

Baklanoff, Eric N. 1971. International economic relations. In Carmelo Mesa-Lago, ed., *Revolutionary Change in Cuba*. Pittsburgh: University of Pittsburgh Press.

Bazsó, C. S. 1975. A kubai külkereskedelem tizenhat eve-a gazdaság politikai változások tükrében (Cuba's foreign trade: sixteen years reflected in economic policy changes). *Világgazdaság* 7, no. 51 (1975), supplement. (Summarized in *Abstracts of Hungarian Economic Literature* 5, no. 1 [1975]: 212–14.)

Bekarevich, A. D., and Kukharev, N. M. 1973. *Sovetskii Soiuz i Kuba: ekono-micheskoe sotrudnichestvo (The Soviet Union and Cuba: Economic Co-operation).* Moscow: Nauka.

Bondarchuk, V. I. 1973. Soviet-Cuban economic cooperation. In P. N. Fedo-seyev, ed., *Sovetskii Soiuz i Kuba: 15 let bratskogo sotrudnichestva (The Soviet Union and Cuba: 15 Years of Fraternal Cooperation).* Moscow: Nauka. Translated as *Cuban Economic Development: Cooperation with CMEA Countries,* JPRS 63185 (10 October 1974), MCUSGP 11568 (1974).

CMEA: Sovet Ekonomicheskoi Vzaimopomoshchi (Council for Mutual Economic Assistance). *Statisticheskii ezhegodnik stran-chlenov Soveta Ekono-micheskoi Vzaimopomoshchi (Statistical Yearbook of the Member Countries of the Council for Mutual Economic Assistance).* Moscow: Stastika. Annual.

EG: *Ekonomicheskaia Gazeta (Economics Gazette).* Moscow. Weekly.

EIU: Economist Intelligence Unit. *Quarterly Report for Cuba, Dominican Republic, Haiti, Puerto Rico.* London. Quarterly.

Faddev, N. V. 1974. *Sovet Ekonomicheskoi Vzaimopomoshchi (The Council for Mutual Economic Assistance).* Rev. ed. Moscow: Ekonomika.

Gladkov, N. 1972. Torgovye otnosheniia SSSR so stranami Latinskoi Ameriki (Economic relations of the U.S.S.R. with the countries of Latin America). *Vneshniaia Torgovlia,* March, 11–15.

Gorbachev, B., and Darynsenkov, O. 1973. Kuba no novem etape (Cuba at a new stage). *Kommunist* 2 (January): 81–92.

Hewett, Edward A. 1974. *Foreign Trade Prices in the Council for Mutual Economic Assistance.* Cambridge: Cambridge University Press.

Gonzalez, E. 1971. Relationship with the Soviet Union. In Carmelo Mesa-Lago, ed., *Revolutionary Change in Cuba.* Pittsburgh: University of Pittsburgh Press.

Kaser, Michael. 1967. *COMECON.* 2d ed. London: Oxford University Press.

Konstantinov, Iu. 1975. Valiutno-finansovoe sotrudnichestvo stran SEV (Mon-etary-financial cooperation of the countries of CMEA). *Voprosy Ekono-miki,* June, 81–89.

Kukharev, N. 1973. Novye rubezhi sovetsko-kubinskogo ekonomicheskogo so-trudnichestva (New frontiers of Soviet-Cuban economic cooperation). *Vneshniaia Torgovlia,* July, 11–15.

Mesa-Lago, Carmelo, ed. 1971. *Revolutionary Change in Cuba.* Pittsburgh: University of Pittsburgh Press.

Mesa-Lago, Carmelo, and Zephirin, Luc. 1971. Central planning. In Carmelo Mesa-Lago, ed., *Revolutionary Change in Cuba.* Pittsburgh: University of Pittsburgh Press.

Rodríguez, C. R. 1971. C. R. Rodríguez interviewed. *Cuba Internacional,* No-vember-December, 86–91. Translated in JPRS, *Translations on Latin America* no. 706 (25 April 1972), MCUSGP no. 8465–18 (1972), pp. 50–62.

———. 1975. Untitled interview. *Ekonomicheskoe sotrudnichestvo stran-chlenov SEV (Economic Cooperation of the Member-Countries of CMEA)* 1:33–34.

Tokareva, P. A., ed. 1972. *Mnogostoronnee ekonomicheskoe sotrudnichestvo sotsialisticheskikh gosudarstv (Sbornik dokumentov, izdanie 2-d, dopolnen-noe) (Multilateral Economic Cooperation of the Socialist States [A Col-*

lection of Documents; 2d Expanded Edition]). Moscow: Iuridicheskaia literatura.

Vladimirskii, V. 1972. Krepnut sovetsko-kubinskie torgovo-ekonomicheskie sviazi (Soviet-Cuban trade and economic relations are strengthened). *Vneshniaia Torgovlia*, October, 14–18.

VT: *Vneshniaia Torgovlia (Foreign Trade)*. Monthly journal of the Ministry of Foreign Trade, also available in English. Moscow: Izvestiia.

Cuban Military and National Security Policies

JORGE I. DOMINGUEZ

Objective Threats to Revolutionary Rule

The history of the first decade of revolutionary rule in Cuba cannot be separated from the history of the threats to its continuation. The history of the second decade of revolutionary rule reflects the complex question of how to control the social and economic burden of national security policies which may have outlived their usefulness, while at the same time projecting Cuban influence overseas.

The Cuban revolutionary government had to build a large and powerful military establishment if it was to survive in the 1960s. The Bay of Pigs invasion of 1961 and the missile crisis of 1962 were but the highlights of a long and violent struggle with the United States. There was substantial covert U.S. support for activities in Cuba against the revolutionary government, including efforts to assassinate Prime Minister Castro, and U.S. policies sought the diplomatic and economic isolation of Cuba. Partly supported by the United States, and partly independent of that effort, there were also large-scale insurgencies in every one of Cuba's six provinces in the first half of the 1960s, resulting in thousands of casualties. Other countries in the Americas, especially in Central America, served as staging bases for attacks on Cuba, thus exposing all of Cuba's long coastline to possible aggression. The Cuban revolutionary government required a substantial air force and navy to guard against invasion; and it required substantial land forces (including internal security police) to defeat the insurrections.[1]

77

Ten to fifteen years later, Cuba's situation had greatly changed. The internal threat had virtually vanished: the last significant insurgencies were put down in 1965, and much of Cuba's "revolutionary vigilance" became a routine function of the civilian Committees for the Defense of the Revolution (CDRs), requiring no military forces or visible display of soldiers and weapons.[2] Collective isolation through the Organization of American States came to an end in 1975, and in the mid-1970s, Cuba's relations with many American countries ranged from correct to very friendly. Most important, U.S. policies toward Cuba had changed substantially by the third quarter of 1975. The U.S. government voted affirmatively to end the OAS policy of isolating Cuba. The U.S. also removed restrictions on trade with Cuba by subsidiaries of U.S.-based multinational enterprises; it ceased withholding foreign aid from third countries trading with Cuba; and it removed sanctions on ships carrying cargo to and from Cuba. The regulations restricting cultural relations between the U.S. and Cuba were eased, and other small public steps were taken. The U.S. also cut back, and perhaps suspended altogether, its support for covert operations in Cuba (possibly excluding intelligence information-gathering in the field). Though statements of Cuban exile organizations support this conclusion, perhaps the most convincing evidence was the Cuban government's interest in, and hope for, improved relations with the United States. If there were still extensive and intensive U.S. covert operations in Cuba, it is doubtful that the Cuban government would have adopted the warm position toward bilateral relations that it has.[3]

In the last quarter of 1975, however, the increase in Cuban participation in the Angolan civil war brought to a temporary end the process of normalization in bilateral U.S.-Cuban relations. Bilateral relations continued to worsen through the beginning of 1976, culminating in President Ford's attack (in Miami on the eve of the Florida presidential primary) on Prime Minister Castro as an "international outlaw."[4] Nevertheless, even as bilateral relations deteriorated over Angola, the First Congress of the Communist Party of Cuba approved a foreign policy resolution welcoming the "positive steps taken" by the U.S. government to improve bilateral relations in 1975; the First Congress noted that it was "not opposed to a resolution of the historical differences" between the two countries; on the contrary, it was "willing to discuss the normalization" of bilateral relations. While in the past Cuban officials have often stated that the complete removal of the U.S. bilateral embargo policy was a precondition for negotiations, the resolution of the First Party Congress opened the door to a bargain somewhat short of that: "Before official discussions . . . begin, it will be necessary for the U.S. . . . to formalize the elimination of the *essential aspects*" of the embargo or, as the Cubans prefer it, the blockade (emphasis mine). Prior to the approval of this resolution, Fidel Castro's main report to the First Congress had expressed "our appreciation" to those who had voted to lift OAS sanctions and had pointedly noted that bilateral relations with the U.S. "would give our country the chance to use many technological advances that are now denied to us . . . and to obtain plants and equipment for our economic plans at lower transportation costs or on better financial terms."[5]

The Carter administration renewed the policy of reconciliation between the United States and Cuba that its predecessor had begun. Both countries fielded diplomats to staff "interest sections" attached to the Czech and Swiss embassies in Washington and Havana, respectively. They signed agreements delimiting overlapping maritime and fishing jurisdictions. Although Cuba terminated the anti-hijacking agreement that both countries signed in 1973 (the agreement expired in April 1977), they developed informal ways to carry out the same policies the agreement had stipulated. The U.S. government prosecuted counter-revolutionary terrorism based in the United States with greater vigor than in the past. Further symbolic steps began, concerning tourism, U.S. prisoners in Cuban jails, and cultural exchanges. The U.S. suspended airplane surveillance of Cuba, relying instead on satellite information. These policy decisions and their implementation altered the political and military nature of the U.S.-Cuban relationship.

Yet this new period of reconciliation also came to an end, at least temporarily, because of the participation of the Cuban armed forces in the war between Ethiopia and Somalia in 1977–78, and perhaps also because of the indirect support that Cuba and Angola may have given to Katanga or Shaba insurgents who invaded Zaire in 1977 and again in 1978. The increased political hostility between the United States and Cuba in the spring of 1978, however, was not accompanied—for the first time in the contemporary history of their bilateral relations—by U.S. military threats against Cuba.

While it is difficult to forecast what implications Cuba's military activities in Africa may have for the defense of the homeland, the extent of the objective threat—from the United States and elsewhere—is now far less than in the past (Watts and Domínguez 1977:16–20).

Cuba and the U.S. Military Posture

In the mid-1960s, the Cuban government was concerned that U.S. foreign policy had taken a virulently aggressive turn. The United States invaded the Dominican Republic and introduced large numbers of U.S.

troops in South Vietnam. In Latin America the U.S. took a strongly anticommunist position, with a distinct anti-Cuban slant. But in the late 1970s, the Dominican invasion has faded into the past. The U.S. is out of Vietnam. And there seems to be little taste among the U.S. public or its leaders for foreign intervention or, indeed, for any kind of foreign policy which might increase the level of U.S. involvement anywhere in the world.

The United States Department of Defense does not consider Cuba a serious threat to U.S. security, though it considers it "some" threat. The North American Air Defense (NORAD) no longer has air defense radar, command and control installations, or weapons in the south central United States. Its capabilities to monitor Cuban activities, and to pose a possible threat to Cuba, are ordinarily limited to those at Homestead Air Base in southern Florida. The Guantánamo naval base has little importance for United States military training; the number of military personnel there in 1975 was about 2,800 (in addition there were some two thousand contractors and about an equal number of dependents). Guantánamo's chief functions were to support U.S. naval operations launched primarily from other bases, to monitor commercial sealanes and Cuban and Soviet activity, and to serve as a strategic bargaining chip. As for possible use of Cuba by the Soviets, the Chairman of the Joint Chiefs of Staff has testified that the "Soviet Union does not currently possess the capability to embark on military aggression in the region." The Soviet Union in the Caribbean poses only a "potential" threat. And the United States could, in theory, mobilize its forces relatively quickly against Cuba. Indeed, the main U.S. defense against a hypothetical Cuban attack is the U.S. ability "to inflict unacceptable damage upon Cuba quickly and decisively from the air and sea." The ordinary disposition of U.S. forces toward Cuba, however, emphasizes monitoring and includes only minimal defense capabilities. These capabilities have been substantially reduced from their high point in the early 1960s.[6] United States military forces are no longer poised to pounce on Cuba, and this fact reflects the basic policy judgment that a military confrontation in the Caribbean, with Cuba or the Soviet Union, has become highly unlikely. Cuba, in turn, has derived security from this judgment.

Cuba's participation in the Angolan civil war, however, raised momentarily the specter of bilateral U.S.-Cuban military conflict. In February of 1976, President Ford "solemnly warn[ed] Fidel Castro against any temptation to armed intervention in the Western Hemisphere. Let his regime, or any like-minded government, be assured the United States would take the appropriate measures." Secretary of State Henry Kissinger subsequently extended the warning beyond the Western Hemisphere, to any additional Cuban military involvement in Africa.[7] And yet the Carter administration refrained from military confrontation of Cuban activities in the Horn of Africa and did not threaten Cuba directly. In sum, the U.S. military threat to continued revolutionary rule in Cuba was negligible by the late 1970s—drastically different from what it had been in the previous decade. Nevertheless, the proliferation of Cuban military participation in African wars, and the increasing U.S. concern with such activities, may eventually lead to a U.S.-Cuban military clash in Africa, either directly or by proxy if both sides are arming and training competing forces.

Cuban Defense Policy and the Role of the Military in Cuban Life

The Cuban government has felt reasonably "secure" since approximately 1965. On 22 January 1965, Prime Minister Castro noted that Cuba had acquired full control over the surface-to-air missiles in its territory; there was no longer any decision-making ambiguity.[8] As noted earlier, the last internal insurgencies of any consequence were also defeated in that year. Nevertheless, in July 1967, Armed Forces Minister Raúl Castro presented two security-related reasons for the maintenance of a large military establishment (in addition to other social, economic, and political reasons of an internal nature) (Domínguez 1974:219–36; and 1976). One was the potential military threat to Cuba from its neighbors, principally from the United States. Raúl Castro reviewed published reports of U.S. military contingency plans, the record of clashes around the Guantánamo naval base, reports of CIA covert operations including plots to assassinate his brother the prime minister, and press reports that the United States had never agreed not to invade Cuba as part of the bargain to solve the 1962 missile crisis. Cuban security, Raúl Castro said, should not rest on U.S. willingness to respect an agreement. He also reviewed possible military threats to Cuba from Venezuela and from other Latin American countries that might be inclined to retaliate against Cuban "solidarity" with revolutionary movements operating in those countries (Castro 1967: 6–12, 19–21). The year 1967 marked the peak of Cuban support for such movements; the meeting of the Latin American Solidarity Organization occurred in Havana in the summer of that year.

The second national security reason given by the armed forces minister for maintaining military strength was the need for self-reliance.

Should the national security, which is our very existence in this case, depend exclusively on foreign support? We think not. Why not? Because that would ill accustom our people to depend on others for the resolution of our problems. Do we have that support? Yes, we do. Is it good? It is. Should we depend on it exclusively? No. [Castro 1967:21]

This cautious phrasing reflected the increasing strain in Cuban-Soviet relations over a host of issues, which reached its point of greatest tension in late 1967 and early 1968. At that time, a "microfaction" was uncovered within the Cuban Communist Party, including its Central Committee, in coalition with Soviet and East European party and government personnel, seeking to change Cuban government and party policy. The Soviet Union slowed down petroleum deliveries to Cuba, so that petroleum products rationing in Cuba had to be tightened severely.[9] At a time of great uncertainty about the quality of Soviet-Cuban relations, the armed forces minister was prudently making a case for Cuban military self-reliance in facing a United States perceived to be still very aggressive (only two years earlier the U.S. had invaded the Dominican Republic, though then preoccupied with Vietnam). Raúl Castro concluded that Cuba would have to sacrifice aspects of its development, especially in construction, to "prepare the country for a war which will begin we know not when." Therefore, the new military budget (300 million pesos, up 50 million from 1967) was the highest of the second half of the 1960s, both in absolute terms and as a percentage of gross national product (5.8 percent in 1968, up 1 percent from 1967), reflecting Cuba's greater commitment to support revolution in Latin America and the greater strain in Cuban-Soviet relations in that year (Castro 1967:22; Domínguez 1976: table 2).

A plausible case can be made that Cuba's national security policy decision, though very expensive, bore some correspondence to the remaining objective threat. By the mid-1970s, however, the direct objective threat to Cuba had declined even further and some aspects of the national security rationale were no longer pertinent. Relations between Cuba and the Soviet Union began to improve after Prime Minister Castro endorsed the Soviet invasion of Czechoslovakia in 1968; they have been very warm ever since (Domínguez 1975a:24–25). While self-reliance may be the determining ingredient of Cuban military doctrine, and a prudent policy in itself, it need no longer be justified by serious doubts concerning the quality of Cuban-Soviet relations.

Relations between Cuba and many other Latin American countries have also improved markedly since 1968. No threat is expected from them. Cuba now counts Venezuela among the politically "independent" countries of Latin America, which it courts assiduously. In the late 1970s, Cuba had diplomatic relations with Argentina, Barbados, Canada, Colombia, Guyana, Jamaica, Mexico, Panama, Peru, Trinidad-Tobago, and Venezuela.[10] Fidel Castro said, for all but the deaf to hear, that Cuba was prepared to suspend all support but symbolic solidarity for revolutionary movements in Latin American countries that have cordial relations with Cuba. Cuba, he noted, has "observed international norms" concerning nonintervention in the internal affairs of other countries which respect such norms with regard to Cuba; Cuba was "willing to go on observing them, as those who also respect them will discover." As for the threat from the United States, it is clear from the preceding sections that it had become rather minor. In fact, Fidel Castro had even outlined a tentative agenda for U.S.-Cuban negotiations once the embargo was lifted, an agenda that included "compensation (the compensation they would demand from us, and the compensation we could demand from them because of the fifteen years of blockade), and the occupation of a part of our territory, the Guantánamo naval base."[11]

Despite these changes in objective conditions, some important themes of Cuban national security policy have changed very little. On 22 November 1974, Prime Minister Castro asserted that "our country will need, . . . over an indefinite period of time, greater and greater defense capacity." The only national security reason given for it had been reduced to the following: "Even if one day there should be economic and even diplomatic relations between us [Cuba and the United States], that would not give us the right to weaken our defense because our defense can never depend on the imperialists' good faith."[12] Seven months later, Armed Forces Minister Raúl Castro stressed the "essential need to increase our military power constantly." He added that the government planned to adhere to this "firm commitment . . . despite the fact that the present correlation of forces favors the socialist camp and despite the positive advances made in international detente."[13]

Foreign policy considerations were not, however, the only reason why Cuba retained such a large military establishment. Possible disputes within the Cuban leadership over the role of the armed forces may involve not only the extent of their overseas use, as we shall see, but also the quality of life in revolutionary Cuba and the role of the armed forces therein. The Cuban military have long been "civic soldiers," fusing civilian and military tasks in a single role, claiming expertise in education, economics, politics, and revolutionary symbolism as well as in the use of force.

What is the context of the debate?[14] After 1970, the Cuban armed forces shifted their less professional personnel to the military reserves and reduced the size of the standing military force from approximately

250,000 in 1970 to approximately 100,000 in 1974. But despite this reduction, the military budget increased in the early 1970s, reaching about 400 million pesos in 1974, as Cuba changed from a labor-intensive to a capital-intensive military. And the decline in personnel was not as great as the figures suggest, since the number of civilians working for the armed forces increased 23 percent from 1971 to 1975. More importantly, the new system of military reserves subjected all men up to the age of fifty, and all women up to the age of forty, to a military classification. Thus every civilian through middle age must become a part-time soldier. Military reserve call-ups may entail as much as three months of military service a year. This military reserve has become the backbone of the national defense. The reserve troops ordinarily account for more than half of the troops participating in war games; the reserves are mobilized for these maneuvers typically for three to four weeks. In addition, a change in the organization of the armed forces, and of the draft laws, established three categories of people. Some would enter the regular units of the military; some would enter the Army of the Working Youth, newly created from units of the armed forces which had been engaged principally in production and from some civilian youth units of what once had been conceived as voluntary labor; and some would remain civilians but serve for three years in a government-designated task. Thus military draft mechanisms are used to allocate young people to the labor supply. These changes have increased the weight of the military on the lives of ordinary Cubans, less because of the increased budget than because the military has come to rely on part-time civic soldiers for the national defense.

The change reflects the belief of some Cuban leaders that the military life should be emulated by all citizens and that participation in some aspects of military life contributes to building the character of the good socialist citizen. For example, a program of regular military training was introduced in the mid-1970s as a part of the civilian senior high school curriculum, with courses conducted by military officers; among the benefits to be promoted by the program were the following: modesty, confidence, honesty, camaraderie, courage, affection and respect for other socialist countries, patriotism, and conscientious discipline. These military teachings would be "among the most important courses" because of their educational and security value.[15]

There is no public debate in Cuba, of course, on the merits of a greater or lesser role for the military in national life. But the persistent references to these issues by the prime minister and the armed forces minister suggest that there is a discussion within the elite ranks. Both Fidel and Raúl Castro have tried to show, for example, that the mobilization of military reserves does not disrupt production because the remaining patriotic workers take up the challenge of higher productivity. At the First Party Congress, Fidel Castro called upon his comrades to "combat the occasionally exaggerated criteria as to who cannot be dispensed with in production";[16] the effect of those "exaggerated criteria" was to reduce the number of people available for military call-up. Presumably those who uphold those criteria are not enthusiastic about the effects of military reserve mobilization on production. There are probably, therefore, a number of elite Cubans who would prefer to reduce the impact of the military on national life, including its impact on production, and who try to alter national policy by an obstructionist interpretation of military call-ups.

However, the argument is not likely to take the form of a simple military-versus-civilian dispute. The need to create the Army of the Working Youth as a specialized branch of the military focusing on production suggests the possibility—not otherwise proven—that some of the more professional officers, seeing the military as a full-time profession, argued that regular units of the armed forces should do no productive work. They may have called for a clearer distinction between military and civilian lives, for a lean, small, well-trained armed force without part-time soldierism. Thus a professional military perspective, in the Cuban context, could be an argument for curtailing the influence of the military on civilians. On the other hand, there are civilians —some of whom were once military men, such as Education Minister J. R. Fernández—who believe that the armed forces ought to have greater weight on civilian life. The same beliefs have been expressed by civilians who were never in the armed forces. For example, the first secretary of the Oriente province party, Armando Hart, has argued that the Army of the Working Youth has made an indispensable contribution to the economy of that province by providing a permanent agricultural work force year-round, even between harvests.[17] Of course, other civilians, perhaps those around Carlos Rafael Rodríguez, may not share these beliefs about the value of the military life in building good citizens or in building an efficient and productive economy.

At the center of the controversy is the role of coercion and hierarchy in a socialist society. The critics of a continuing military demand on civilians may support some foreign military activity such as the training of the troops of friendly countries, but measured in dozens of persons, not in tens of thousands such as those sent to Africa for combat. They may also argue that, in the absence of a credible threat to the continuation of revolutionary rule in Cuba, fewer citizens should be coerced through the draft laws; and that the hierarchical life style of the military is inappropriate for a socialist society. In this view, military stratification in civilian life has no intrinsic value, and many costs.

The Overseas Spread of the Cuban Armed Forces

The African phase of Cuban military affairs has added new dimensions to Cuban national security policies. Fidel Castro's main report to the First Party Congress in December of 1975 noted that "the starting point of Cuba's foreign policy, according to our Programmatic Platform, is the subordination of Cuban positions to the international needs of the struggle for socialism and for the national liberation of peoples." This statement was followed by a long section professing Cuba's foreign-policy loyalty to the Soviet Union. The foreign-policy resolution of the First Congress reaffirmed that Cuba "subordinates its interests to the general interests of the victory of socialism and communism, of national liberation." Lest there be any confusion about the role of China, the First Congress noted that "State relations have been developing normally" with Albania and China, "from which we are separated—primarily—by their well-known international positions, condemned in the Declaration of the Communist Parties of Latin America, in terms that the Congress expressly ratifies." Early in 1976, relations with China worsened as a result of divergences over policies toward Angola; Cuba charged that imperialism, racism, and Maoism were cooperating to snuff out the national liberation of Angola, through the combined actions of the U.S., South Africa, and China. Finally, both the prime minister and the First Congress committed themselves specifically and open-endedly to participate in the Angolan civil war.[18] Therefore, in addition to the hypothetical threat to Cuba which heretofore had justified the existence of a large military establishment, there was a new justification for such policies: the present and future commitment to send the Cuban armed forces to fight overseas.

Although Cuba had, in the 1960s, actively supported revolutionary movements in many countries, those commitments had never been formally tied to the role and purpose of the Cuban armed forces. Cubans who had fought abroad, expressing their international duties and commitments, were said to have acted on their own, though with the warm support of the Cuban people, party, and government. Thus, for example, Ernesto (Che) Guevara had renounced formally all his positions in Cuba before embarking on his career as a revolutionary in Bolivia. Never before had the Cuban armed forces been formally committed to overseas combat; never before had overseas combat been a formal part of their military mission. There is, consequently, a new, additional rationale for the Cuban armed forces which is not merely related to national defense. Engagement in overseas combat is now rewarded publicly and explicitly within Cuba. Prime Minister Castro noted that this was one of the criteria on which individuals might be judged worthy to enter the Central Committee of the Cuban Communist Party. At the First Party Congress in 1975, 8 percent of the 3,116 delegates present had won merits for their active participation in actions of international solidarity.[19] The constraints on Cuba's ability to commit troops overseas are tightening, but they do not yet seem sufficient to deter Cuba from continuing its African operations. One possible constraint, Cuban internal politics, appears so far to permit further military operations. Some members of the top elite, who may be more interested in using foreign policy to advance Cuba's internal economic development than in advancing revolution elsewhere, do not ordinarily speak out for larger military commitments, at home or abroad. They (including Vice-President for Foreign Affairs Carlos Rafael Rodríguez) are typically silent on these issues, even though they may realize that Cuba is being burdened by military commitments abroad. On the other hand, the budgetary constraint on Cuba may be increasing. Although Cuba has received its weaponry from the Soviet Union free of charge, it has incurred many direct military costs. From the eve of the Angolan war to the eve of the Ethiopian war, the declared military budget doubled, reaching 784 million pesos budgeted for 1978;[20] and the actual expenses incurred in 1978 will probably be substantially higher as a result of the Ethiopian war. Cuba did not have to invest its weaponry in Angola or in Ethiopia; the Cuban forces were transported to both countries equipped with light arms, and heavier weapons were supplied on the spot by the Soviet Union. But much of the transportation of Cuban troops, albeit slowly, inefficiently, and dangerously, was done by Cuban civilian aircraft and merchant and shipping fleets (Domínguez 1978a). More importantly, notwithstanding Soviet economic support, Cuba has had to commit some of its best people to the African wars even though Cuba's personnel resources are limited. One result may have been a more pronounced economic crisis in Cuba than might otherwise have occurred.

In the mid-1970s, the Cuban economy finished its best sustained economic performance since the prerevolutionary period. The average rate of growth for gross product was approximately 10 percent between 1971 and 1975; because of the drop in the world price of sugar that began in late 1974, the average growth rate was forecast to fall to 6 percent from 1976 to 1980. In fact, gross product grew only 3.8 percent in 1976 and about 4 percent in 1977[21]—both years when the world economy was recovering and the world price of sugar had begun to stabilize, but both following Cuba's entry into the Angolan war and subsequent engagement in protracted guerrilla warfare in Angola. There are, of course, many factors that might account for the drastic decline in the economic growth rate; one would be mistaken to attribute the decline solely, or even primarily, to the Angolan war. But that war no doubt is part of the reason why the Cuban economy has performed much less well in the second half of the 1970s. The Ethiopian war can only compound the economic burden of Cuba's military policies.

Additional costs have been incurred by the Cuban armed forces as an institution. Although most Cubans probably supported participation in the African wars, the evidence from the Angolan war alone already suggested civilian resistance to military mobilization, as well as incidents of troop insubordination (Domínguez 1978b). Wars have costs in lives and resources that bear hard on military and civilian morale. Cuba's African wars are no exception; in fact, the war in support of Ethiopia and against Somalia may have been costlier than the Angolan war. Although the Cuban government has not revealed the number of casualties, the official explanation of the victory in the Horn of Africa noted that Somali soldiers were "tough and fought bravely." Fidel Castro added that they had shown "real fighting spirit."[22]

The more sustained impact of overseas war on Cuba, of course, is felt through the substantial reliance on military mobilization for overseas combat. Approximately 70 percent of the troops that fought in Angola were reservists. The military response to the Angolan war was thus to increase the size of the reserves and their military preparedness and professionalism.[23]

If the internal constraints on Cuban foreign policy have been increasing very slowly, Cuba has set for itself certain major guidelines for the conduct of its foreign military policy (Domínguez, forthcoming). Cuban policy has been to assure all Latin American and black African countries, regardless of ideology, against an invasion carried out by the Cuban armed forces. This marks, of course, a departure from Cuban activities in the 1960s, when ideological differences, especially in Latin America, were likely to trigger some kind of Cuban effort to penetrate other countries. Che Guevara's adventure in Bolivia was the prime example of that now defunct policy. In this respect, then, Cuba's policy, despite the direct involvement of the armed forces overseas, has some new limitations, albeit modest, that it did not have in the 1960s. However, the range of opportunities that Cuba has left open for itself, especially in Africa, is extensive.

Cuban foreign policy permits several kinds of military involvement abroad. First, Cuban armed forces may be sent into front-line combat to repel a conventional military invasion of one country by another. This is Cuba's official rationale for its support of Ethiopia against Somalia in the 1977–78 war. This is the language of high diplomacy, rather than merely the language of revolutionary solidarity. The concern is less with the quality of the incumbent regime than with the defense of borders and territorial integrity; strategic concerns and political influence take primacy over the promotion of the good society abroad. Second, the Cuban armed forces may be sent into combat overseas to help an incumbent government suppress an insurrection described as the result of foreign intervention. The Cuban-Angolan military treaty, signed in 1976, commits Cuba to the unlimited defense of Angola against hostile neighbors who are alleged to be the central cause of protracted resistance to Luanda's rule. Although Cuba had begun withdrawing some troops from Angola in 1976, the internal war was re-escalated in April 1977 and fresh Cuban troops went into combat to support the Neto government.[24] Third, the Cuban armed forces may provide training and supplies to forces in one country, for the host country's and Cuba's own purposes; and the trainee forces may then, at a later time, invade another country without additional Cuban participation. This apparently occurred in the case of the invasion of Zaire's Shaba province in 1977 and 1978.

Cuba's assurances against military invasion are not extended to the white governments of Rhodesia and South Africa. Against them, all features of Cuban policy, from support of subversion to the use of regular troops, remain conceivable. There are also no assurances in North Africa, where Cuban support for the Algerian-based Polisario guerrillas against Morocco, Mauritania, and France could escalate into major warfare.

Central Elements of Cuba's Policy Today

The main elements in Cuba's military and national security policy can be stated in seven major propositions. First, the policy depends on some kind of détente with the United States, because the U.S. remains the chief threat, and because reconciliation may eventually reduce the costs of Cuba's national security measures. Second, in the absence of more than modest change in U.S.-Cuban relations, a substantial Cuban military establishment is still necessary, pending more concrete bilateral agreements. Third, Cuba must continue to align itself closely with the

Soviet Union to obtain military, political, and economic protection without which the Cuban Revolution could not survive. Fourth, Cuba continues to expect some unconventional attacks from exile groups. Fifth, the continued large internal security apparatus suggests that the government is still concerned about internal unrest. Sixth, Cuba has retained an unconventional capability to advance its political goals, through contacts with revolutionaries the world over. And seventh, Cuba retains a substantial military establishment able to implement foreign policy decisions, in close alliance with the Soviet Union, and to support allied incumbents abroad by providing a broad array of services, including front-line combat and logistical forces. The provision of these services to third countries cements the Soviet-Cuban alliance and increases Cuba's worth to the Soviet Union.

Cuban national security depends in large part on a perception by the U.S. government that Cuba poses no significant danger to U.S. security. The most important possible threat to stable U.S.-Cuban relations would be a major increase in the role of Cuba as a support for the Soviet navy. The Soviet Union has been making slow changes in the type of submarine calling at Cuban ports, testing the limits of U.S.-Soviet agreements with regard to the use of Cuba as a Soviet "base."[25] At present, no part of Cuba serves as an operational base from which the Soviet Union could mount an attack on the United States; should Soviet use continue to increase at the present rate, that would continue to be the case. The chief effect of the pattern of Soviet use, present and projected, would be to establish the political and military "right" of the Soviet navy to patrol the Caribbean, but without military capabilities to launch an attack from there.

A secondary threat to the U.S. is Cuba's bomber aircraft force, composed of older airplanes, MiGs from the first post-World War II generations.[26] This bomber force has been gradually phased out, with the possible effect of reassuring the United States that Cuba lacks an autonomous offensive capability and that no credible threat is posed to the United States from the Caribbean.

The second of the seven propositions—maintenance of a large military establishment—is a necessary consequence of the lack of fulfillment of the first—U.S.-Cuban détente. Cuba has sought to deploy a capability to inflict considerable damage on a U.S. invading force, so that thousands of U.S. troops would be killed. This "bee-sting" capability may well be too high a price for any U.S. government to pay in the foreseeable future. The maintenance of a substantial military capability has also required, as the third proposition indicates, the continuation of excellent relations between Cuba and the Soviet Union, within limits not threatening to the United States. The presence of Soviet advisors, equipment, and some ships in Cuba serves as a "trip wire": an invasion of Cuba cannot help but destroy Soviet personnel and property, hence involving the Soviet Union in the dispute automatically. In addition, Soviet economic assistance to Cuba has been essential for the survival of revolutionary rule. A discussion of the extent of such assistance would take us far afield, but it is plain that the material underpinnings of Cuban national security would be devastated without Soviet support. Close alignment with the Soviet Union remains an indispensable pillar of Cuban national security policy, entirely independent of any joint overseas actions undertaken by these two countries.

Unconventional warfare, primarily from Cuban exiles but also from other bands which have traditionally operated in the Caribbean, remains an active threat to Cuba, for whose deterrence Cuba retains its fighter/interceptor aircraft force, as well as its patrol boats equipped with short-range, surface-to-surface missiles. The navy and a substantial part of the air force provide the essential forces for this aspect of Cuban national security. The anti-aircraft defense is also of obvious importance here. While the Guantánamo naval base is unlikely to be used for conventional war, it does hold a potential for unconventional war; thus army forces deployed near the base are also necessary.

Cuba has not only been the target of unconventional warfare, but also has engaged in it, because this was long the only available means of defense against its enemies. Cuba sought to increase the cost to the United States of supporting U.S. clients, especially in Latin America. Because of changes in the international environment, as well as the requirements of Cuban internal development, the policy of support for unconventional warfare abroad has been curtailed substantially. But these capabilities are still used to some degree against enemy governments, such as Chile and Rhodesia. Cuba's modest support for Puerto Rican independence also falls under this rubric.

A related issue has been the pursuit of intelligence information. This has been responsible for some of Cuba's more serious foreign policy setbacks in the 1970s, such as the "Carlos affair" in France. The Cuban leaders and agencies dealing with foreign and economic policy had made a concerted effort, during the first half of 1975, to improve political and economic relations with France. Cuban undercover agents, in the meantime, maintained close relations with South American, Palestinian, and other terrorist groups operating in Paris. The discovery of these links led to the expulsion from France of three Cuban diplomats in July 1975. This was a serious setback for Cuba's main policies toward France, and suggests poor coordination within the Cuban foreign policy bureaucracy.[27]

In addition to the provision of combat troops for Angola and Ethiopia discussed in the preceding section, Cuba already had a substantial foreign aid program, including foreign military aid. On the whole, the Cuban foreign aid program differs from the programs of other countries in that Cuba sends personnel to perform certain tasks, whereas other countries ordinarily transfer financial resources. Because Cuba has few funds to give, it has preferred to transfer people. For example, Cuba has sent construction workers to build schools, hospitals, and other buildings for civilian and military purposes in Peru, Guinea, North Vietnam, Jamaica, and Tanzania.[28] Cuba has sent dozens of teachers to Spanish-speaking Guinea.[29] Cuba has had military assistance programs in Syria, Southern Yemen, Congo, Somalia (until 1977), Algeria, Guinea-Bissau, and, of course, Ethiopia and Angola.[30] Cuba has also supported extensively and for military purposes such countries as Vietnam, Laos, Cambodia, and Guinea. These programs have been conducted over a number of years, without seriously impairing Cuban foreign relations; the close coordination of current programs with the Soviet Union, moreover, serves the dual purpose of strengthening Cuban-Soviet relations (tacitly repaying a part of Cuba's debt) and of providing Soviet political cover for Cuba's program.[31]

Prospects for the Future

Cuba's foreign military policy has come to play a major role in the affairs of that country and in the affairs of a great many other countries. From the savannahs of Angola to the deserts in the Horn of Africa, Cuban armed forces have emerged victorious in short, quick wars. The future, however, holds for them the prospect of protracted warfare in Angola and, depending on the evolution of their commitment to Ethiopia, perhaps there as well. Cuban actions against Rhodesia and South Africa have escalated with time; and the likelihood of a confrontation between Cuba, on the one hand, and France and Morocco, on the other hand, from the western Sahara to south central Africa has been increasing. At home, the weight of the armed forces on the social system has been rising, too, through budgetary costs and especially through the establishment of claims on the lives of citizens, who will have to serve in the armed forces in larger numbers and for longer periods of time.

This essay has eschewed a detailed discussion of political-diplomatic considerations, especially relations with the United States. Nevertheless, U.S.-Cuban relations will determine the degree and quality of Cuban national security in the years to come. I have discussed U.S.-Cuban political-diplomatic relations in some detail elsewhere (Domínguez 1973, 1975a, 1975b; Watts and Domínguez 1977).[32] However, two aspects of that present and future bargaining have specialized implications for the Cuban armed forces: the post-détente military link to the Soviet Union, and the status of the Guantánamo naval base.

The status of Guantánamo is never mentioned by the Cuban leadership as a precondition to meaningful bargaining with the United States. It is never mentioned as something Cuba expects to discuss in the near future after negotiations are launched. But it is often mentioned by most of the leadership (except principally those dealing with international economic relations) when a long-term, complete agenda for U.S.-Cuban relations is discussed; and it is always mentioned by Fidel and Raúl Castro in this context. Thus the fact that this issue will be a part of the long-term bilateral agenda cannot be ignored. Apart from symbolic and political value, the base also requires the commitment of a part of Cuba's military and internal security forces; indeed, it provides the only need for land forces for external defense apart from the possibility of a sea-borne invasion. Thus the issue of the base is not only a foreign policy matter; its return to Cuba would also affect the role of the Cuban military and the balance of power within the armed forces.

It is important to the Cuban armed forces that no settlement with the United States deny them access to Soviet weaponry, technical assistance, and training. That seems to be the *sine qua non* of military-bureaucratic requirements. Apart from that, it is possible that the Cuban armed forces could endorse the curtailment of Soviet naval visits to Cuba as a part of an overall, complex settlement, so long as there were no threat to the military lifeline from the Soviet Union.

In sum, the Cuban Revolution has survived difficult years. It has defeated internal and international opponents. There is no longer a serious direct threat to Cuban national security, even though a national security case for a Cuban military establishment can still be made. Since the fall of 1975, however, Cuba has come to be perceived, in many ways for the first time, as a conventional military threat to other countries. Whether the future will show a feedback effect on Cuban national security as a result of the Angolan and Ethiopian expeditions, only time will tell. At any rate, the rationale for Cuban military policies has been modified to include—besides a residual problem in bilateral relations with the United States at a military level—a commitment to have troops available for conventional overseas service. There is also a profound internal reason for the preservation of a large and weighty military establishment—the belief of some Cuban leaders that the military makes a unique and positive contribution to the development of the good socialist citizen. The forthcoming debate in Cuba is likely to include, therefore, two distinct themes. One is the fate of the civic soldier; the other is whether there should be two, three, or many Angolas and Ethiopias. The forecast is that those who wish to curtail the internal and international role of the Cuban armed forces will lose.

Acknowledgments

An earlier version of this paper was presented at the Conference on the International Relations of the Cuban Revolution, sponsored by the Ibero-American Language and Area Center at New York University, 31 October and 1 November 1975. I am grateful to the participants in that conference for their comments and criticisms. I am also grateful to the Center for International Affairs at Harvard University for making this research possible.

This paper has been concerned neither with the totality of Cuban foreign policy nor with the entire role of the armed forces in Cuban society, but with the much narrower question of policies formulated at the interface between foreign policy and military policy. This deliberate narrowing necessarily implies a certain loss in richness and complexity. Nevertheless, the more delimited subject matter of this essay remains important in itself; since the topic has been underresearched, the present analysis may be useful.

Notes

1. Most of the events described here are common knowledge. I have attempted to assess the internal impact of these events, in terms of casualties, budgets, and manpower, in "The Civic Soldier in Cuba" (Domínguez 1974). Subsequent releases, however, make it clear that the published data of the U.S. government, on which I had relied, seriously underestimated Cuban military expenditures in the early 1960s. Whereas published U.S. government data suggested annual average expenditures between 210 and 225 million pesos in the early 1960s, Fidel Castro has now revealed that the correct statistic is much closer to 500 million pesos. Therefore, the peak proportion of gross national product devoted to military purposes was probably not the previously calculated 8 percent, but between 16 and 20 percent. For the higher statistic, see Mankiewicz and Jones (1975:118).

2. For the activities of the Committees for the Defense of the Revolution—often aimed at common crime rather than counterrevolution—see "Tarea no. 1 de los CDR: Vigilancia revolucionaria," *Con la Guardia en Alto* 7 (December 1968); and Lezcano (1975).

3. See Prime Minister Castro's response to the partial lifting of the U.S. embargo in *Granma Weekly Review*, 31 August 1975, pp. 7–8, where he outlines a possible agenda and set of procedures for negotiations; see also his answers to Mankiewicz and Jones (1975:126–56).

4. *New York Times*, 29 February 1976, p. 1.

5. *Granma Weekly Review*, 25 January 1976, p. 10, and 4 January 1976, p. 11.

6. U.S. Armed Services Investigating Subcommittee (1972:35–37, 41, 57); "The Pentagon's Appraisal of the Latin American Situation," *Inter-American Economic Affairs* 29, no. 2 (Autumn 1975):91–92, 94.

7. *New York Times*, 29 February 1976, pp. 1, 42.

8. *Revolución*, 22 January 1965, p. 4.

9. On the microfaction, see *Verde Olivo* 9, no. 5 (4 February 1968):4–6, and the full supplement to that issue; see also "Informe del Comandante Raúl Castro ante el Comité Central" (conclusion), "Intervención del compañero Carlos Rafael Rodríguez en la reunión del Comité Central," and "Informe del fiscal en el juicio seguido a Aníbal Escalante y 36 acusados más," all in *Verde Olivo* 9, no. 6 (11 February 1968). On the petroleum slowdown, see *Granma Weekly Review*, 7 January 1968; and Mazin (1967:15–16).

10. For a summary of Cuba's diplomatic range see *Bohemia* 67, no. 23 (6 June 1975):83.

11. *Granma Weekly Review*, 31 August 1975, pp. 7–8.

12. *Ibid.*, 1 December 1974, p. 7.

13. *Granma*, 11 July 1975, p. 2.

14. The following paragraphs summarize a more detailed discussion in Domínguez 1978a: ch. 9.

15. *Granma Weekly Review*, 23 March 1975, p. 4.

16. *Ibid.*, 4 January 1975, p. 7.

17. *Granma*, 5 August 1975, p. 3.

18. *Granma Weekly Review*, 4 January 1976, pp. 10–11, and 25 January 1976, p. 10; see also 11 January 1976, pp. 4–5. On worsening relations with China, cf. *Granma*, 27 January 1976, p. 1.

19. *Granma Weekly Review*, 11 January 1976, pp. 2–3; *Granma*, 25 December 1975, p. 1.

20. *Granma Weekly Review*, 6 August 1972, p. 4; 4 January 1976, p. 7; 1 January 1978, p. 3.

21. *Ibid.*, 28 December 1975, pp. 5, 8, and 1 January 1978, p. 2.

22. *Ibid.*, 26 March 1978, p. 5, and the special *Granma* supplement circulated with this issue and dated 14 March 1978.

23. *Verde Olivo* 18, no. 6 (6 February 1977) :10.

24. See summary of discussion between President Castro and congressmen Fred Richmond and Richard Nolan: "Representatives Fred Richmond and Richard Nolan, Discussions with Cuban President Fidel Castro," a mimeographed document available from Hon. Fred Richmond, U.S. Congress, House, p. 9.

25. See the useful discussion in U.S. Subcommittee on Inter-American Affairs (1974).

26. For the number and kind of the main Cuban weapons systems, mentioned here and in other paragraphs, see Domínguez 1976: table 1.

96 / Jorge I. Domínguez

27. *Granma Weekly Review*, 25 May 1975, p. 3. *Le Monde*, 16 January 1975, pp. 1, 4; 4 July 1975, pp. 1, 24; 11 July 1975, pp. 1, 8. *The Times* (London), 11 July 1975, pp. 1, 6; 12 July 1975, p. 2.

28. *Granma*, 6 December 1975, p. 4; *Granma Weekly Review*, 12 October 1975, p. 2.

29. *Granma Weekly Review*, 4 November 1973, p. 7; 24 February 1974, p. 5; 29 September 1974, p. 1. Also Crozier (1975:9); *New York Times*, 3 March 1976, p. 4; and *Boston Globe,* 15 February 1976, p. 49.

30. *Granma Weekly Review*, 11 January 1976, p. 5.

31. For a general discussion, see Domínguez, forthcoming.

32. See also U.S. Subcommittees on International Trade and Commerce and on International Organizations (1976:101–03).

References

Castro, Raúl. 1967. Graduación del III curso de la escuela básica superior "General Máximo Gomez." *Ediciones al Orientador Revolucionario* no. 17.

Crozier, Brian. 1975. The Soviet pressure in Somalia. *Conflict Studies* no. 54 (February).

Domínguez, Jorge I. 1973. Taming the Cuban shrew. *Foreign Policy* no. 10 (Spring).

———. 1974. The civic soldier in Cuba. In Catherine M. Kelleher, ed., *Political-Military Systems: Comparative Perspectives*. Beverly Hills, Calif.: Sage Publications.

———. 1975a. Cuba, the United States and Latin America: After détente. *SAIS Review* 19, no. 1.

———. 1975b. U.S. policy toward Cuba: A discussion of options. In *The Americas in a Changing World*. New York: Quadrangle.

———. 1976. Institutionalization and civil-military relations in Cuba. *Cuban Studies* 6, no. 1 (January).

———. 1978a. *Cuba: Order and Revolution*. Cambridge, Mass.: The Belknap Press of Harvard University Press.

———. 1978b. The Cuban operation in Angola: Costs and benefits for the armed forces. *Cuban Studies* 8, no. 1 (January).

———. Forthcoming. The armed forces and foreign relations. In Cole Blasier and Carmelo Mesa-Lago, eds., *Cuba in the World*. Pittsburgh: University of Pittsburgh Press.

Lezcano, Jorge. 1975. Informe central presentado al pleno. *Con la Guardia en Alto* (third series) 14, no. 4 (April).

Mankiewicz, Frank, and Jones, Kirby. 1975. *With Fidel*. Chicago: Playboy Press.

Mazin, A. 1967. Trade brings peoples closer together. *Current Digest of the Soviet Press* 19, no. 50.

U.S. Armed Services Investigating Subcommittee, Committee on Armed Services, House of Representatives. 1972. Cuban plane incident at New Orleans. *Hearings.* 92nd Congress, 1st Session, 9 and 17 November and 9 December 1971. Washington, D.C.: Government Printing Office.

U.S. Subcommittee on Inter-American Affairs, Committee on Foreign Affairs, House of Representatives. 1974. Soviet activities in Cuba. *Hearings.* 93rd Congress, Parts 4 and 5, 31 October 1973 and 20–21 November 1974. Washington, D.C.: Government Printing Office.

U.S. Subcommittees on International Trade and Commerce and on International Organizations, Committee on International Relations, House of Representatives. 1976. U.S. trade embargo of Cuba. *Hearings.* 94th Congress, 1st Session, 8, 13, 15, 20, and 22 May, 11 and 26 June, 9 July, and 23 September 1975. Washington, D.C.: Government Printing Office.

Watts, William, and Domínguez, Jorge I. 1977. *The United States and Cuba: Old Issues and New Directions.* Policy Perspectives, no. 1. Washington: Potomac Associates.

Why Cuba Is in Angola
(and What's Next)

ABRAHAM F. LOWENTHAL

AUTHOR'S NOTE: *I drafted the following essay early in 1976, shortly after the massive Cuban intervention in Angola became known. At the time, most commentators were attributing the Cuban move either to bald Soviet imposition or to a reversion by Cuba to the erratic romanticism of the Che Guevara period. My essay used the device of an imaginary Cuban internal memorandum to make the point that one could, using techniques similar to those employed by our own national security managers to calculate the "national interest," plausibly account for the Cuban decision to enter the Angolan conflict. The essay attempted to set out the operating premises of Cuban policy as I understood them, and to reason from those premises. Since that time, versions of the article have been published in* O Estado do Sao Paulo *(May 1976) and in* International Security *(Summer 1977).*

Much has happened in Africa since the time this essay was first drafted. Cuban soldiers not only have aided the triumph of the Popular Movement for the Liberation of Angola (MPLA), but have stayed in Angola more than three years already. (The hypothetical advisers' comment that a "protracted" struggle might prove costly may be more than a little prescient!) Jimmy Carter was elected president of the United States and began a process of rapprochement with Cuba. And, most important, Cuban troops have turned up in several African countries besides Angola, notably in Ethiopia.

The extensive Cuban military involvement in Africa, especially the Cuban role in Ethiopia, raises important questions about Cuba's policy, questions which may illuminate the Angolan episode in retro-

spect. Thus, although my imaginary Cuban advisers could plausibly emphasize in 1975 that in Angola "we believe that Cuba has a rare opportunity to pursue most of its foreign policy objectives simultaneously, at little cost," by now it is evident that Cuba may undertake military activities in Africa even when substantial costs are involved. Disaffection within the Organization of African Unity and within the "nonaligned" movement, a cooling of relations with Venezuela and other Latin American nations, a virtual suspension of U.S. moves toward rapprochement—these and other costs have not deterred Cuba from its Ethiopian and other African involvements.

If I were writing a new article on Cuba's African policy, I would have to consider these realities and many other complex issues of fact and interpretation. I would have to begin with a careful study of what the Cubans are actually doing and what they are not doing in various sites—published reports diverge considerably—and then I would have to try to analyze the relationship between Cuban interests and perceptions and those of the Soviet Union.*

Neither time nor data permit me to prepare such an essay now. At the editor's request, therefore, I present below the unaltered text of my original essay. I do so with some discomfort, for the essay did not accurately forecast what Cuba has actually done in Africa since 1976; it assumed that Cuba's withdrawal from Angola had begun and it did not anticipate Cuba's extensive involvement in Ethiopia. Still, even taking these important flaws into account, I believe that the central line of reasoning presented in the hypothetical memo has held up well. Whatever the pressures and cross-pressures, it has become increasingly evident that Cuba's own perceptions and stakes—not merely Soviet dictates—bear very importantly on Cuba's foreign policy decisions. That being so, the heuristic device of outlining Cuban interests and reasoning about them becomes even more useful as the nature of Cuba's interests in Africa becomes more complex.—A. F. L.

Several thousand Cuban soldiers—as many as fourteen thousand, according to Secretary of State Kissinger—are now in Angola, six thousand miles from Havana. At least a thousand more are elsewhere in Africa and the Middle East. That much is clear, and surprising.

Cuba's sudden and substantial entry into Angola last fall sparked intense speculation in many quarters about Cuba's international role and intentions. Some reports depicted Cuba as a helpless paw of the Russian bear, supplying shock troops to advance Soviet imperial designs. Others suggested that Cuba was willingly collaborating with the

---

*On these points, I am indebted to Peter Winn and Carla Robbins.

Soviet Union but that the initiative for Cuba's Angolan thrust must have come from Moscow. Still others asserted that Cuba had undertaken its bold action in Angola largely on its own. They suggested that Fidel Castro was trying to infuse Cuba's foreign policy with renewed revolutionary fervor, reverting in some measure to the days of Che Guevara and dropping his earlier apparent interest in establishing relations with the United States. Fear mounted, at least in some circles, that future Cuban policies would be dangerously "destabilizing." Visions were conjured up of Cuban "gurkhas" swarming all over Africa. Remarkably vague American threats were issued about the dire consequences Cuba might suffer if it committed its forces beyond Angola: in Rhodesia or Namibia, especially.

Then, just as suddenly as the major Cuban forces had appeared in Angola, reports began to circulate that they were beginning to leave. Cuba's deputy prime minister told reporters in Tokyo that Cuba had no intention of sending its forces to Rhodesia; he held out the hope, perhaps not coincidentally, for Cuban rapprochement with the United States after the November elections in this country. Fidel Castro himself, in a letter to Sweden's prime minister, apparently committed Cuba to withdraw its troops from Angola. Some in Washington, not least among them the usual "senior official" on Secretary Kissinger's plane, began immediately to credit themselves with having brought about a reversal of Cuba's policy. *Time*'s report on Angola (June 7), for instance, crowed, "Castro: Pressure Begins to Work."

Why did Cuba send combat forces to Angola? What role did the Soviet Union play in making the decision to introduce soldiers there? Why are the Cubans beginning to withdraw? To what extent has Cuba reversed the policy it was originally pursuing in Angola, and why? Is Cuba still likely to send its troops elsewhere in Africa, or even in the Caribbean, as some have speculated? If not, what accounts for Cuba's seemingly erratic behavior, for what the *San Juan Star* calls "Fidel's changeable mind"? Has Washington's bluster caused Cuba to change its course, or has it perhaps caused Russia to modify Cuba's policy?

In analyzing Cuba's Angolan venture and in thinking about what may happen next, it is worth speculating that Cuba's actions in Angola —both its entry and its incipient withdrawal—may have resulted neither from Soviet pressure nor from unbridled Cuban romanticism eventually reversed by American threats, but rather from consistent, hard-headed, and realistic calculations of Cuba's national interests.

Consider, for example, the following imaginary memorandum from unnamed Cuban foreign policy advisers to Fidel Castro. It is dated last September, when the Cuban decision to intervene in Angola on a major scale was probably made.

September 15, 1975

Fidel Castro

Mr. Prime Minister:

You have requested that we analyze the consequences of expanding Cuba's military involvement in Angola from the present level of a few hundred advisers to the several thousand combat troops requested by Agostinho Neto of the MPLA.

We understand that unless Cuba sends combat troops, the MPLA will probably be defeated before the national independence date of November 11, in part because of overt South African and clandestine U.S. support for the factions opposed to Neto's movement. Our long support for Neto's movement would have proved of no avail.

We also understand that substantial Cuban military involvement will almost certainly produce a quick victory for the MPLA against the lightly armed and poorly organized anti-MPLA forces.

We have kept in mind these two premises as well as all the major objectives of Cuba's foreign policy: (1) to protect the Cuban Revolution; (2) to support the just cause of national liberation movements elsewhere and to strengthen international solidarity among anti-imperialist forces; (3) to preserve the benefits of our close alliance with the Soviet Union while increasing our own autonomy in international affairs; (4) to strengthen our political and commercial ties with the countries of Latin America and the Caribbean; (5) to support nonviolent Third World efforts to change the terms of relations between our countries and the industrial world; (6) to expand Cuban access to advanced technology from capitalist sources and to markets in the capitalist world; and (7) to move toward mutually respectful relations with the United States of America, Cuba's nearest potential market and the best source for much of the technology this country requires.

Sometimes taking an action to advance one goal retards or reverses progress toward another, forcing eventual choices among them. In this case, however, we believe that Cuba has a rare opportunity to pursue most of its foreign policy objectives simultaneously, at little cost. We are even inclined to believe, contrary to what some *compañeros* have argued, that participating in the Angolan struggle will not significantly alter the prospects for normalizing relations with the United States.

Our reasoning follows:

(1) Protecting the Cuban Revolution

Sending several thousand troops to Angola will not expose the Revolution to any grave risk.

At home, the Revolution is now fully consolidated, supported by the vast majority of Cubans and fortified by our many recent economic and political successes. A protracted and losing war in Africa might ultimately be dangerous. But quick and successful participation in the Angolan struggle will bring pride to Cuban homes, even to those who must, inevitably, bear sacrifices in this cause.

The United States will be upset by our expanded engagement, no doubt, but there is no indication that the ruling circles in the United States have a major stake in Angola, and the North American reaction is not likely to be dramatic.

Even if the United States should react strongly, we believe that the Americans will be powerless to stop our engagement. Because of its long-standing commercial embargo of Cuba, the United States has long since deprived itself of the chance to exert any significant leverage against us, short of outright acts of war; now it can only embargo the hope of an eventual resumption of trade. In the aftermath of Vietnam, the United States will be unable to gain national support for any direct action in Angola. It is even doubtful, given recent developments in congressional-executive relations, that the United States will be able significantly to increase its covert action there. And it will surely be unable to mobilize international support for multilateral measures against us, particularly in the light of South Africa's involvement.

We must ask whether the North American capacity for international adventurism is still such that the United States government might try to harm Cuba directly in response to our action in Angola. We think this risk is minimal, both because the international balance of power has shifted so considerably in recent years, and because U.S. public opinion has changed.

(2) Supporting National Liberation Movements

Our support for the MPLA will strengthen proletarian internationalism in the worldwide fight against racism, colonialism, and imperialism, for the MPLA's victory will affect the correlation of forces all over southern Africa. The presence of Cuban forces in Angola will encourage the national liberation forces of Zimbabwe, Mozambique, and Namibia, and it will discourage South Africa from direct intervention in any of these struggles. The bankruptcy and internal contradictions of U.S. policy in Africa will reveal themselves. In its desire to oppose the Soviet Union and Cuba, the United States will be tempted—against the will of some within the U.S.A.—to align itself ever more closely with the white racist regimes of Rhodesia and South Africa. If and when the United States tries to disassociate itself from these regimes, it will hasten their demise.

Our role, moreover, will mark Cuba as a courageous and principled country at the very vanguard of the anti-imperialist movement. That earned reputation will help Cuba avert criticisms if and when we feel it in our interest to make a number of pragmatic concessions in our relations with the United States.

(3) Strengthening Cuba's Alliance with the U.S.S.R. While Increasing Our Own Autonomy

Although we can immediately send several hundred men to Angola in Cuban ships, a truly large-scale operation would require airlifting men and materiel. The Soviet Union has already indicated its willingness to provide air transport, furnish equipment on the ground, and absorb certain foreign-exchange costs.

Cuba's response to Neto's request will please the Soviet Union, our closest ally. It will also remind the authorities in Moscow, however, of our independent capacity to promote armed struggle abroad; in the past, we have successfully used this capacity as a bargaining counter in our own relations with the Soviet Union. Our response will also tend to engage the Soviet Union more extensively in the national liberation struggle, thus encouraging the U.S.S.R. to play a role more appropriate than the conservative one it played in Vietnam. It should be noted, by the way, that the People's Republic of China has been involved with the Angolan factions opposed to the MPLA; by supporting the MPLA, we will also be administering a defeat to Chinese adventurism.

In addition, our autonomy in international affairs will be considerably enhanced if we can make our aid responsible for the national liberation of an oil-exporting country. We will continue to rely on the Soviet Union for petroleum at a preferential price, but it may be useful to develop friendly relations with other oil exporters.

(4) Strengthening Cuba's Ties with Latin America and the Caribbean

Although we will gain closer relations with some of the English-speaking Caribbean countries because of our forthright stand against racism in Africa, we may also offend some of our current or potential allies, including countries —such as Venezuela, Colombia, Costa Rica, and Peru—with which we have only recently resumed relations. Some sectors, particularly in the armed forces, will fear our potential to "export revolution," even in this hemisphere.

We must be very careful, therefore, to assure those selected Latin American governments with which we wish to have correct or cordial relations that our involvement in Angola does not forbode intervention in this hemisphere. We should note that we are responding to a request from the best-established and most widely recognized force in Angola, which seemed likely to win control of the country before South Africa and the United States intervened. We should stress, for instance, that Brazil had already decided to recognize the MPLA as Angola's government. And Cuba should emphasize that it is not participating in efforts at violent subversion against existing governments.

Had the question of aiding the MPLA come up before mid-1975, while the OAS sanctions against Cuba were still in effect, it would have been much more difficult to proceed in Angola. We would have feared then that the arguments for maintaining a politically inspired embargo would have been reinforced. Now that the embargo has been lifted and we enjoy mutually advantageous commercial and political relations with a number of Latin American and Caribbean states, we can afford the risk of a temporary cooling in some of these relations. For the governments of Latin America to return all the way to a policy of isolating Cuba would contradict their own political interest in asserting independence of Washington and their economic interest in trade and in "collective self-reliance."

(5) Strengthening Third World Solidarity
and Bargaining Power

Our audacious and successful support for the MPLA will enhance the Third World's solidarity and self-confidence. This subjective power will translate into objective force in the various international forums where negotiations are being conducted on issues ranging from agricultural commodities to Zionism.

(6) Increasing Cuban Access to Advanced Technology
and Expanded Markets in the Capitalist World

Cuba's role in Angola need not retard our increasingly successful efforts to gain access to Western markets and technology. It is possible that we will lose some ground politically, but the countries of Western Europe and Japan will not stop trading with us because of our activities in Angola.

(7) Normalizing Cuba's Relations with
the United States

Now that the U.S. presidential campaign has begun in earnest, we believe there will be no further steps toward normalizing relations until early 1977 at least, no matter what we do in Angola. Indeed, President Ford's rivalry with Ronald Reagan for the Republican nomination, and the central place of the Florida primary in Reagan's campaign strategy, may well lead Ford to take a hard line on Cuba in any case. This factor may well account for the U.S. government's decision to ignore our many positive gestures toward rapprochement and to insist on maintaining the hostile apparatus of the unilateral trade embargo.

We think our engagement in Angola in 1975–76 will not substantially and adversely affect the chances for improving Cuban-American relations in 1977–78, at least not unless President Ford is elected or Governor Reagan becomes president, contingencies we regard as unlikely and extremely unlikely, respectively.

Assuming that a Democrat is elected, a new president may use the Cuban issue to dramatize his innovative policies. Even if not, a number of specific interests in the United States—mainly those with goods to export or technology to license—will begin to pressure for renewing U.S.-Cuban relations. By then, that sector of the increasingly divided Cuban American community still opposed to rapprochement will no longer be so influential, for it will be a long time before the votes of Cuban Americans will be of such national significance again.

By 1977 or 1978, our participation in the Angolan struggle in 1975–76 will not seriously restrict the chances for normalization of relations. The American public as a whole, which no longer reads or hears anything about Indochina, will have soon forgotten about Angola. The foreign-policy-making elite in the United States will remember Angola, but they will realize that our action there illustrates the cost to the United States of ignoring Cuba. American foreign policy specialists will argue that U.S. policy toward Cuba has not encouraged restraint on our part because it has not provided any incentive to us for choosing one course as opposed to another.

In summary, we recommend that Cuba respond promptly and positively to Neto's request for combat troops. To do so is correct, it will advance the causes of socialism and national liberation in Africa, it will benefit Cuba in a number of different ways, and it will not involve any serious risk of major adverse consequences.

I have no idea whether a memorandum like this exists in Havana. Even if it does, it may well rationalize a decision really taken (probably incrementally) for other reasons ranging from personal whim to bureaucratic or factional struggle. In any case, the memorandum's reasoning may itself be criticized. The strength of the North American and even the South American reaction to Cuba's action may well have been underestimated, for instance. The discussion of Cuba's relations with the Soviet Union may have exaggerated Cuba's autonomy, a failure of self-perception probably common, in some degree, to all international actors. The discussion of what Agostinho Neto's MPLA represents may have exaggerated the movement's programmatic and ideological nature and minimized its ethnic and factional base, for the tendency to imbue essentially local and factional struggles with international ideological significance is not limited to American officials.

Still, in analyzing the apparent Cuban decision not to expand Cuba's military involvement in Africa but rather to begin withdrawing its forces from Angola, we should consider the possibility that Cuban officials weighed the costs and benefits in the same judicious manner the imaginary memorandum conveys.

The same foreign policy advisers who recommended sending Cuban troops to Angola would probably argue convincingly against Cuban combat involvement elsewhere in southern Africa. They would emphasize that the risks to Cuba of such involvement in another case are bound to be much higher than those faced in Angola, and that Cuba's gains would be substantially smaller. Among their arguments would be these:

(1) In Angola, Cuba was invited by the strongest nationalist movement, with which Cuba had been allied for over a dozen years. Elsewhere in Africa, Cuba has no such clear alliance, and some of the national liberation forces (in part under Chinese influence) even oppose Cuban intervention.

(2) Elsewhere in southern Africa, Cuban forces might have to face well-trained, well-armed, and highly motivated South African and Rhodesian soldiers.

(3) The Soviet Union might hesitate to jeopardize its relations with the United States and Western Europe by extending its African engagement.

(4) Governor Reagan's success in the primaries increases the possibility that the United States might find some way to implement its publicly implied threat to punish Cuba for any further intervention in Africa.

(5) The prospect that Cuban involvement could precipitate racial war in southern Africa might engage European attention and could jeopardize the vital commercial credits Cuba has secured in Europe.

(6) Further Cuban military involvement in Africa might strain or even crack African and Third World solidarity, especially because some of the major African countries might resent Cuban intervention.

(7) A further Cuban military venture would probably significantly exacerbate antagonism to Cuba within Latin America.

(8) Prospects for eventual rapprochement with the United States would be notably dimmed if Cuba undertook a "second Angola" in defiance of the United States.

(9) Most of the gains Cuba might achieve have already been secured by the Angolan triumph, and would not be multiplied by a second or third intervention, even a successful one.

Basing their analysis on reasoning like this—not on fear of American reprisal for Angola or on sudden shifts of policy—Cuban foreign policy makers might very well have decided that Cuba should "quit while it's ahead," consolidate its influence in Angola, and limit its involvement in national liberation movements elsewhere in southern Africa to providing training, advice, funds, and encouragement. Cuba, no doubt, regards Angola as a triumph for its foreign policy, and it may believe that dignified withdrawal now will preserve Cuba's victory.

Cubans in the United States:
Their Impact on U.S.-Cuban Relations

LOURDES CASAL

At the time of the 1970 Census, the number of Cubans living in the United States, considering nationality both by birth and by parentage, was approximately 613,000. This was a corrected estimate excluding Puerto Rico (Prohías and Casal 1973:25). By 1976, taking into account birth and death rates and the influx of Cubans from Spain, we can estimate that the number had risen above 750,000—a figure that includes Puerto Rico. This would make Cubans the third-largest Spanish-speaking minority in the United States. Moreover, given their concentration in the Miami area,[1] they have become the principal Spanish-speaking group in the American South, just as Mexican Americans predominate in the Southwest and Puerto Ricans in the Northeast.

The particular characteristics of the Cuban immigrants make them a special group, with special problems and needs and special relations to U.S. policies. The Cuban migration has taken place over a fairly concentrated period of time; its remote cause has been clearly political; it has brought to the United States a group that is rather atypical among immigrant populations; and it has involved the United States for the first time in a complex refugee operation that has cost the country over a billion dollars in direct disbursements. To date, the full dimensions of the situation have rarely been explored. This paper will begin by discussing the demographic characteristics of the Cuban exiles, then will examine their politics and ideology and their impact, both actual and potential, on U.S. domestic and foreign policy.

The Demographic Facts

The Cubans in the United States are an overwhelmingly urban group concentrated in a number of *colonias* (settlements) in major metropolitan areas. Miami, Florida, is the site of the largest settlement, containing roughly half of the U.S. Cuban population. The second-largest *colonia*, encompassing about one-fourth of the Cubans, is located in the New York metropolitan area, with subunits in the Washington Heights–Inwood section of Manhattan, Jackson Heights in Queens, and Elizabeth and West New York–Union City in New Jersey. The remaining quarter of the population is scattered throughout other areas, including Los Angeles, Chicago, Boston, and New Orleans.[2]

Thus, instead of discussing the Cuban community, we should speak in many cases about the Cuban communi*ties*, the different *colonias* which are sometimes very small and situated in areas of clear Anglo predominance. But the sheer size and concentration of the Miami community should not be forgotten. Miami Cubans are frequently considered to represent U.S. Cubans as a whole, even though their political spectrum, influenced by a right-wing ethnic press, may be far narrower than those of other *colonias*.

The total number of Cuban immigrants since 1959 is impossible to calculate precisely. The figure of 750,000 mentioned earlier is this author's best recent estimate. However, no agency is in charge of keeping count of all Cubans entering the country; though the Cuban Refugee Program[3] has come closest to fulfilling that function, not all Cuban immigrants have registered with the CRP. Cubans have come in indirectly through third countries and with a variety of statuses under the immigration laws, such as "parolee," "resident," and "tourist." The 1960 Census, taken when the migration had just begun, included 124,416 individuals of Cuban birth or parentage. The 1970 Census's equivalent number was 560,628, but an undercount of Cubans (as well as other minorities) has always been suspected. To reach the figure of 613,000 quoted earlier for 1970, Prohías and Casal (1973:17) estimated the undercount to be 9.3 percent.[4] For comparison we can cite the Cuban Refugee Program's calculation, which would place the total size of the migration up to 1976 at approximately half a million. This estimate, because of the incompleteness of CRP registration, is certainly a minimal figure.

STAGES OF THE MIGRATION

First stage: January 1959 to October 1962, the period of regular airline flights between Cuba and the United States. Until 3 January

1961, when diplomatic relations between Cuba and the United States were broken, prospective emigrés could secure visas at the U.S. embassy in Havana and the Santiago de Cuba consulate. After that date, immigrants began to use the "third country" route, traveling first to Spain, for example, where they could apply for entry visas. Soon, however, the U.S. Department of State, together with the Department of Justice, began the visa-waiver procedure, allowing the visa requirements to be set aside in "emergency" cases. The term "emergency" was rather liberally interpreted: Monsignor Walsh, who in his position as bishop of the Miami diocese was a central figure in organizing the program for unaccompanied children, has recently acknowledged that his operation was granted "blanket authority to issue visa waivers to all children between the ages of six and sixteen" (Walsh 1971:402).

Second stage: October 1962 to 1 December 1965. This stage began with the suspension of regular flights between the United States and Cuba in the aftermath of the October missile crisis. The migration rate slowed: Cubans resorted to the "third country" route and to "unconventional means" such as small boats. Premier Castro's speech of 28 September 1965, inaugurated the chaotic Camarioca period, in which hundreds of boats left Miami for the Cuban port of Camarioca to pick up relatives of Cubans already in the United States. No clear estimate exists of the number of people who migrated under such conditions.

Third stage: 1 December 1965 to April 1973. After the signature of a Memorandum of Understanding between the Cuban and U.S. governments, a special airlift operated between Varadero and Miami. This continued with varying degrees of regularity throughout the period.

Fourth stage: April 1973 to the present. When the airlift ended, the migration was reduced to a trickle. A limited number of migrants still arrived through third countries, but from April 1973 through 1975 most of the Cubans entering the United States were emigrés who had been waiting in Spain for their visas. The U.S. Immigration and Naturalization Act had originally provided preferential treatment for aliens from the Western Hemisphere by exempting them from the fixed quotas applied to other nationalities. An amendment of October 1965, by ending the quota system, eliminated the preferential treatment and created a bottleneck for the Cubans in Spain. The difficulty was compounded in July 1968 by the imposition of an overall limit of 120,000 persons a year for natives of independent countries in the Western Hemisphere. This limit, together with the other provisions of the Immigration Law—such as the preference given immediate relatives of citizens, and those with professional status or skills in demand—made entry nearly impossible for those who had chosen the Spanish route. In spite of considerable lobbying by Cuban groups in the United States, it was not until late 1973 that special provisions were made to admit the estimated 20,000 Cubans in Spain.

During the early fall of 1978, Cubans who could claim dual citizenship (having been born in the U.S. or of U.S. parentage) were granted exit visas. Also, as part of a general process of rapprochement between the Cuban regime and the Cuban community in the U.S., large numbers of political prisoners were given visas to emigrate to the United States.

THE IMMIGRANTS' REPRESENTATIVENESS

Several investigators have been concerned with the question of "representativeness"—that is, to what extent do Cuban exiles represent the different strata of Cuban society? Cuban migrants, as a whole, are not a representative sample of prerevolutionary society. Table 1 compares figures on occupational categories from several samples of Cuban exiles with corresponding figures from the 1953 Cuban census. Fagen, Brody, and O'Leary's sample of Cuban Refugee Center registrants up to March 1963 showed professional, semiprofessional, and managerial persons overrepresented by a factor of more than four, while persons in extractive occupations (agriculture and fishing) were underrepresented by a factor of about 14 (1968:19). The overrepresentation of the upper strata of Cuban society is also evident in the educational distribution data: while only 4 percent of the Cuban population, according to the 1953 census, had completed twelfth grade or above, 36 percent of the Refugee Center refugees were so classified (p. 19).

However, there have been marked changes over time. The Fagen, Brody, and O'Leary data in the table refer primarily to the migrants of the first stage. After the Bay of Pigs incident, the exodus doubled its rate and was characterized by a different occupational mix. The data of Fagen and his colleagues indicate that the emigration of middle-level professional and clerical workers may have risen at this time (1968:64–66). According to Clark (1970:10–12), the shift may have been pronounced: the arrivals by "unconventional means" during the second stage overrepresented young adult males, and almost half of the total were skilled and semiskilled workers.

Because of the airlift regulations,[5] third-stage refugees overrepresent students, children, and housewives (Thomas 1967:53). And from the "Late Refugees" column in Table 1, it is apparent that the employable 1965–1966 refugees included a markedly greater proportion

Table 1 / Occupational Distributions of Cuban Emigrants Compared to Distribution of Cuban Population in 1953

Pre-exile Occupations	Cuba, 1953[a]	Miami, 1963[b]	"Unconventional Means" Arrivals[c]	Late Refugees, 1965–1966[d]	Indianapolis, 1966[e]	Resettled Refugees, 1966[f]	West New York, 1968[g]
Professionals, managers, proprietors, technicians	9.2%	37%	18.1%	21.4%	69.6%	46.5%	44.9%
Clerical and sales	13.7	31	11.7	31.4	21.7	18.7	24.1
Skilled, semiskilled, and unskilled	27.2	20	49.0	32.9	8.7	34.8	16.2
Extractive	41.7	3	10.7	4.8	0.0	0.0	0.0
Services	8.3	9	10.5	9.5	1.0	0.0	13.7

[a]$N = 1,938,228.$

[b]Fagen, Brody, and O'Leary 1968; $N = 55,354.$

[c]Clark 1970; $N = 10,632.$ The sample was taken in 1968 but most of these refugees can be assumed to have arrived during the second stage (October 1962 to 1 December 1965).

[d]University of Miami 1967; $N = 16,587.$

[e]Prohías 1967; $N = 23.$

[f]Wenk 1968; $N = 256.$ The figures have been recomputed to show male respondents only, excluding students, unemployed, and cases in which no information was obtained.

[g]Rogg 1970; $N = 226.$

Table 2 / Age Distribution by Ethnic Origin, March 1972

Age	Total Population	Spanish Origin			
		Total*	Mexican	Puerto Rican	Cuban
Under 5 years	8.5%	12.7%	13.4%	14.0%	4.9%
5 to 9 years	9.2	13.8	15.0	14.7	11.6
10 to 17 years	16.0	19.4	20.2	21.5	13.4
18 and 19 years	3.6	3.8	4.3	2.6	3.8
20 to 24 years	8.4	7.8	8.3	8.0	3.7
25 to 34 years	12.9	14.2	13.3	14.8	13.8
35 to 44 years	11.0	11.8	10.8	12.6	15.4
45 to 54 years	11.4	8.0	7.5	5.3	14.5
55 to 64 years	9.2	5.0	3.9	4.6	12.1
65 years and over	9.7	3.5	3.2	2.0	6.8
Median age (years)	28.0	20.1	18.6	17.9	34.1
Number of persons (in thousands)	204,840	9,178	5,254	1,518	629

*Includes other persons of Spanish origin, not shown separately.

Source: U.S. Department of Commerce 1972.

of the lower occupational sectors than did the emigrés of the early years.

Taken all together, the demographic studies of Cuban migrants in terms of their society of origin indicate that, unlike the typical immigrant populations, the Cubans show an overrepresentation of the upper occupational strata. However, the migrant population is heterogeneous in terms of its occupational mix and there has been a relative increase in lower strata among later exiles.

SOME DEMOGRAPHIC CHARACTERISTICS

Age. Table 2 summarizes the age distribution of Cubans in the United States compared to other Spanish-speaking groups and the total U.S. population, according to a March 1972 sample survey of the Bureau of the Census. The median age for U.S. Cubans of 34.1 is higher than the median age for the U.S. population at large (28.0) and is almost twice the median ages of the other two principal Spanish-speaking groups; Mexican Americans have a median age of 18.6 and Puerto Ricans 17.9. A random sample of Cuban alien registrants as of January 1972, taken by the Cuban Minority Study, shows that the Florida Cuban population tends to be even older than indicated by the Census estimates. Roughly 10 percent of Florida's Cubans are 66 or older; and an additional 19 percent are between 51 and 65 (Prohías and Casal 1973:33).

Race. The black and mulatto populations of Cuba are seriously underrepresented among Cubans in the United States; estimates place them at 4 to 6 percent of the total group (Rogg 1970:150; Prohías and Casal 1973:35).

Sex. A 1971 Current Population Report of the Census Bureau (U.S. Department of Commerce 1971) estimated the sex distribution of Cubans in the United States as 50 percent male, 50 percent female. But a random sample of Florida's Cubans (those registered as aliens in 1972) led to an estimated female-to-male ratio of 1.22 to 1 (Prohías and Casal 1973:34).

Location. The Cuban population in the United States is overwhelmingly urban, and more specifically, metropolitan. Ninety-five percent of the Cubans in the country (excluding Puerto Rico) are living within the Standard Metropolitan Statistical Areas (SMSAs) of the twenty states with the highest Cuban populations. Actually, the concentration of Cubans in particular metropolitan areas is much greater than this figure indicates. Roughly six SMSAs account for 80 percent of all U.S. Cubans: Miami, New York City, Jersey City, Newark, Los Angeles–Long Beach, and Chicago (Prohías and Casal 1973:36).

Naturalization Rate. Naturalization rates are important on a number of practical and theoretical grounds. They are an index of integration or assimilation into U.S. society; and although they can be affected by opportunistic considerations (such as ease of travel and job requirements), naturalization implies a willingness to modify some aspects of the definition of the self, to assume a different loyalty, and to treat the commitment to the United States, at least to a certain degree, as permanent. Furthermore, naturalization rates are important data in judging the political clout at the local and national levels that can be exercised by Cubans—citizenship being, of course, a prerequisite for voter registration and participation in party politics.

The number of naturalizations grew slowly from 1959 to 1969, when it reached roughly 9,000 per year. In 1970, thanks to changes in the Immigration and Naturalization Law, the number of naturalizations jumped to nearly 21,000. From 1970 to 1975 it remained high, averaging roughly 16,000 per year.

ECONOMIC ADJUSTMENT

The story of Cubans in the United States has usually been told as one of unmarred success. Theirs has been described as a "golden" exile (Portes 1969); Cubans are frequently mentioned as having "made it" and articles about the Cuban prosperity have often appeared in the U.S. press. For example, *Business Week* (1 May 1971, p. 88) asserted that Cubans "have made faster progress in their adopted country than has any other group of immigrants in this century."[6] The U.S. agencies involved in the refugee operation (the departments of State and Health, Education and Welfare) have been interested, for reasons of both domestic and foreign policy, in emphasizing the success story,[7] and U.S. Cubans have found it self-satisfying and useful to stress their achievements. Indeed, because of the special characteristics of Cubans as an immigrant group (occupational and educational background, skills, and so on) and the extensive and expensive refugee assistance program,[8] success has been a significant part of the Cuban resettlement.

But the emphasis on the "success story" is now perceived as counterproductive by some sectors of the U.S. Cuban community, because it has prevented Cubans from getting a clear picture of their true situation (cf. Prohías and Casal 1973:7–8); it has desensitized Cubans and the surrounding community to the hidden costs of "success," and it has tended to isolate the Cubans even further from other U.S. minorities.

Though data on economic adjustment are relatively scarce, there is some sample survey information comparing the income distribution of Cubans with that of other Spanish-speaking groups and the U.S. population at large. Table 3 summarizes the pertinent information for March 1972. Cubans fall much closer to the general U.S. population than do the other two main Spanish-speaking groups. Over 21 percent of all Cuban families—compared to 5 percent of the Puerto Rican families and 9 percent of the Mexican American—have incomes of $15,000 or more. Also, there are considerably fewer Cuban families classified in the "low income" categories than there are Puerto Rican or Mexican American families.

The difference is also reflected in the median incomes: $9,371 for the Cubans, compared to $6,185 for Puerto Ricans and $7,486 for Mexican Americans. And a later sample survey suggests that Cubans are increasing their incomes faster at least than Puerto Ricans: in 1975 Cuban median income had risen to $11,410, Puerto Rican median income to $7,629, and Mexican American to $9,500.[9]

However, these income differentials reflect, at least partially, the greater incorporation of Cuban women into the labor force and their contribution to the combined family income. Table 4 summarizes the

Table 3 | Yearly Family Income in 1971 by Ethnic Origin

Total Money Income	Total Population	Spanish Origin			
		Total*	Mexican	Puerto Rican	Cuban
Under $3,000	8.3%	13.8%	14.9%	16.9%	7.9%
$3,000 to $3,999	4.8	8.2	9.2	11.0	3.2
$4,000 to $4,999	5.4	8.4	7.1	10.6	11.3
$5,000 to $5,999	5.7	8.1	8.3	10.2	8.0
$6,000 to $6,999	5.5	7.2	7.0	7.7	3.5
$7,000 to $7,999	6.2	8.0	7.1	12.8	7.6
$8,000 to $9,999	12.3	13.8	15.1	9.9	11.8
$10,000 to $11,999	12.5	11.9	11.8	10.6	15.1
$12,000 to $14,999	14.4	10.4	10.2	5.1	10.2
$15,000 to $24,999	19.5	9.4	8.6	4.5	20.6
$25,000 and over	5.3	0.9	0.5	0.8	0.8
Number of families (in thousands)	53,296	2,057	1,100	363	170
Median family income	$10,285	$7,548	$7,486	$6,185	$9,371
Families whose head is year-round, full-time worker: Median family income	$12,436	$9,596	$9,472	$8,235	$11,296
Percentage of all families	63.5%	57.0%	57.5%	50.7%	61.8%

*Includes other persons of Spanish origin, not shown separately.

Source: U.S. Department of Commerce 1972.

information concerning labor force participation for women. Since women of Spanish heritage in Florida can be considered almost exclusively Cuban, those in the Southwest almost entirely Mexican American, and those in the mid-Atlantic states overwhelmingly Puerto Rican, the table demonstrates that Cuban women have the highest participation rate in the labor force of these three groups. In March 1972, 54 percent of all women of Cuban origin were in the labor force, while only 36 percent of the Mexican Americans and 25 percent of the Puerto Ricans were so engaged. The participation rate for Cuban women is in fact higher than for white women as a whole (42 percent). The high Cuban rate is maintained regardless of child rearing. For

Table 4 / Impact of Child Rearing on the Labor Force Participation of Women

	Labor Force Participation Rates for Women with:		
	Children Under 6	Children Aged 6 to 17 only	No Children Under 18
Total women:			
White	28.4%	49.0%	41.5%
Negro	47.6	59.8	43.4
Women of Spanish heritage:	28.4	43.5	41.7
5 southwestern states	29.8	43.3	40.1
3 mid-Atlantic states	16.6	30.5	39.9
Florida	38.6	59.7	45.1

Source: U.S. Department of Labor 1973:98.

example, even Cuban women with children under 6 years of age have a higher participation rate (38.6 percent) than Mexican American women in general (U.S. Department of Labor 1973).

This situation has latent costs that are not often discussed. The rapid integration of Cuban women into the labor force, coupled with the absence of adequate day-care facilities and the frequent role reversal between parents and children—the children being more competent in the new language, and therefore being relied on for contacts with the outside society—has placed considerable strain on traditional Cuban family patterns. One result has been a high degree of intergenerational conflict.

Other information, gleaned from the 1970 Census and the U.S. Budget, documents the darker side of the story. For instance, one out of five metropolitan Cubans lives in an area designated as "low-income" by the Census Bureau. Again, there are wide regional variations; more than half the Cubans in Newark and Boston inhabit such areas (Prohías and Casal 1973:73). As another instance, at the end of 1972 90,700 persons were receiving financial or medical assistance under the Cuban Refugee Program.[10] The regional figures show that while only 7 percent of New Jersey's Cuban population received aid, 20 percent of those in Los Angeles did.

As a final comment on the deceptiveness of Cuban economic "success," we should note that the Cuban median income in 1975 of $11,410 was still considerably short of the median for the entire U.S. population, $12,836.[11]

OCCUPATIONAL STATUS

It is helpful to consider occupational status separately from economic data, although the two obviously are closely related. Given the over-representation of professional sectors among the exiled population, certain authors (e.g., Thomas 1967) have spoken of the Cuban "brain drain" and how it has benefited the United States. Conversely, from the viewpoint of Cuba, the migration has represented a sizable loss of human capital. But the extent to which Cuban manpower has been well utilized in the United States is debatable. Certain professional groups, with skills in great demand in U.S. society, have fared extraordinarily well: among them are roughly 2,500 physicians who have either obtained their U.S. licenses or are practicing in settings (such as state hospitals and the Cuban "clinic" system in Miami) where licenses are not required. Lawyers, on the other hand, have fared poorly, affected by complex licensing requirements and the radical differences between Cuban law, with its Roman-French-Spanish tradition, and U.S. law, rooted in the Anglo-Saxon tradition (see Moncarz 1969).

Besides these variations according to professional group, there are marked occupational differences according to geographic location. There are areas, such as Puerto Rico, in which migration biases have produced a concentration of upper-class and upper-middle-class Cubans —entrepreneurs, salesmen, media specialists, and other professionals who have re-established and even improved upon their occupational positions in their society of origin. On the other hand, there are areas, like Los Angeles or West New York, where sizable numbers of the Cuban community have experienced catastrophic losses in terms of occupational status.

Table 5 shows the occupational distributions of three samples of Cubans taken in different cities at slightly different times. If these U.S. occupational distributions are compared to those of the same groups of migrants before they left Cuba (Table 1), we can see a loss of occupational status even in the Indianapolis sample. In the Miami 1966 sample, the percentage of workers in the professional, proprietor, technician, and manager categories suffered a four-to-one reduction, while the percentage in the unskilled labor category doubled. In the West New York community studied by Rogg (1970), the Cuban immigrants had suffered an even more marked loss of occupational status than Miami refugees. Rogg described the "enormous downward mo-

Table 5 / Occupations in the U.S. of Three Samples of Cubans

Occupation	Miami, 1966[a]	West New York, 1968[b]	Indianapolis, 1966[c]
Unemployed	11.3%	4.4%	—
Business and Professional	10.5	4.8	56.6%
White-collar	22.6	10.8	—
Blue-collar	17.3	67.6	43.5
Manual	32.3	6.8	—
Other	6.0	5.6	—

[a]University of Miami 1967; $N = 768$.

[b]Rogg 1970; $N = 348$.

[c]Prohías 1967; $N = 23$.

bility that refugees holding middle and higher level occupations have experienced in the U.S." (p. 275). Actually, with the exception of craftsmen, whose skills show maximum transferability, 70 percent of those in Rogg's West New York male sample were working as factory operatives.

The above must not be construed to suggest that the Cuban migrants or their host communities have experienced loss of income. In Miami and West New York, two centers of great Cuban concentration, the impact of Cubans has been beneficial to the local economy, helping to prevent the rapid dilapidation of the central city area characteristic of U.S. cities. As for the Cubans themselves, a sizable number, especially in Miami, have been able to establish their own businesses—although these are usually very small and cater exclusively to the Cuban community. Estimates of Cuban-owned businesses range from 4,500 to 6,000 —both figures probably unreliable. But there are, of course, those who have made it very big: for example, David Egozi, the head of a shoe-making company (Suave) which grossed nearly $43 million in sales in 1970; he sells his shoes to chains such as Woolworth's, and his personal worth is estimated at over $8 million.[12] However, the Egozis are not typical of the Cuban community, as the data we have presented clearly indicate. With the exception of Puerto Rico, there has been a sizable waste of human capital among Cuban exiles.

Political Characteristics of the Exiles

When we move from demographic characteristics to the politics and ideologies of the exile communities, we find a dearth of systematic information. We can, however, make some tentative generalizations, beginning with the basic stages of development (cf. Díaz 1970, 1974).

STAGES OF POLITICAL ACTIVITY

First stage: January 1959 to October 1962. The initial stage was characterized by intense militancy and support for military activities against Castro, including those involving the U.S. government. The primary example was the Bay of Pigs invasion, but there were various raids both before and after.

Second stage: October 1962 to approximately 1965. In this period there were fragmented and uncoordinated acts of hostility—infiltration, sabotage, and the like—against the Cuban regime. The Consejo Revolucionario (Revolutionary Council), the umbrella group that coordinated groups for the Bay of Pigs invasion, disintegrated. The Cuban revolutionary government managed to eliminate guerrilla activity within the island, and the U.S. strategy toward Cuba became one of restrained hostility—containment, isolation, propaganda, and the fostering of internal dissent. The exile groups became adjuncts and instruments of this policy.

Third stage: 1965 to 1969. New militant anti-Castro organizations emerged, but they involved progressively fewer members of the U.S. Cuban communities. Among the majority of the exiles, private issues such as job training and improvement of living standards took precedence over participation in political activities.

Fourth stage: 1969 (a somewhat arbitrary date) to the present. In the current stage the depoliticization of large masses of the exile population has become more apparent. But the Cuban communities have become increasingly heterogeneous: while the majority of the exiles are involved in private concerns, some polarized sectors of the youth have leaned toward radical action. The following sections will discuss the major trends in more detail.

THE DEACTIVATION PROCESS

The highly belligerent movements of the 1960–1964 period, although they never actively engaged the entire exile population, managed to mobilize the financial or moral support of the majority. They embodied the exiles' hopes for the overthrow of the revolutionary regime and a return of the emigrés to Cuba. As these organizations failed to reach their goal—and the international situation plus the internal consolidation of the Cuban regime made it progressively more unlikely that they would—the Cuban communities became disenchanted with such activities and withdrew their support.

Occasionally special "plans" or "programs" still emerge, claiming to have a formula for overthrowing the Cuban regime. But they tend to be ignored by a majority of the Cuban population, which takes a rather skeptical view, since plans of this sort have typically succeeded only in providing financial advantages for the planners. An example is the controversy in several exile communities about the monies collected for the Plan Torriente.[13] José de la Torriente, originator of this plan, was assassinated in his Coral Gables home by a sniper in April 1974.

TERRORISM FROM THE RIGHT

Despite the overall depoliticization of the exiles, some highly belligerent movements still persist: for instance, Abdala, Comandos Libres Nacionalistas, Acción Sindical Independiente, and Alpha 66. With the exception of Abdala, which engages in propaganda and penetration of student and cultural groups, these movements seem to involve rather small numbers of people. There is no mistaking, however, the disruption such right-wing groups have caused: Miami was practically transformed into a city at war when the bombing activities reached peaks in December 1974 and December 1975.[14]

Although extreme right groups have attempted to coordinate their activities under the banner of the Frente de Liberación Nacional Cubano, what characterizes the terrorist activity is the great number of groups or "groupuscules" that claim responsibility for an action and then are not heard of again. Probably the violent actions are carried out by the same persons under different names, to give the impression of a large variety of terrorist groups and to protect some of the major ones, which have above-ground components, from the police and other investigative agencies.

A group that calls itself Zero has claimed credit for assassinating José de la Torriente in April 1974 and Rolando Masferrer in October 1975.[15] (Masferrer was a prerevolutionary strongman who commanded a private army against the revolutionaries during Batista's regime.) Other groups have offered their names in connection with the bombings of the Dominican consulate,[16] the Dominican airline, and the Bahamas airline. The assassination of Luciano Nieves, who openly advocated peaceful coexistence with the Cuban revolutionary regime, was claimed in February 1975 by the Cuban Justice Movement, a group about which nothing had been heard before and nothing has been heard since. Along with claims and counterclaims, accusations abound. A communiqué from one terrorist organization accused the

F.B.I. of Masferrer's death. And some spokesmen from the Miami Cuban community have tried to link terrorism in the city to Castro's agents.[17]

Some terrorist attacks can be seen to have a certain logic, although in the end they are ineffective or even counterproductive.[18] In this class are the attacks directed against Cuban diplomatic missions abroad, or against persons, groups, and institutions perceived as somehow supporting the Cuban revolution (e.g., Luciano Nieves, the Center for Cuban Studies in New York, the Bahamas airline). However, a sizable number of the bombings and assassinations seem either pointless, related to struggles between the groups themselves, or connected with shady financial deals, possibly involving drugs and the Mafia.[19] From coherent (if unsuccessful) strategies in the early days of exile, the Cuban right-wing groups seem to have degenerated into meaningless violence.

Since the fall of 1976, moreover, there has been a major change in the situation of terrorist groups. The assassination in Washington of Orlando Letelier, former Chilean ambassador to the United States, on 2 September 1976 had important repercussions. The ensuing investigation revealed that members of a "nationalist" Cuban group headquartered in New Jersey had acted as agents for the Chilean security police. Evidence was also uncovered that Cuban groups had been involved in other violent acts against enemies of the Chilean junta. Shortly after the Letelier murder came a second event with significant effects: on 6 October 1976 a bomb exploded aboard a Cubana airplane off the coast of Barbados, killing all the passengers and crew, over 100 people. The U.S. government was impelled by these events to take a firmer stand against the terrorists. During 1977 and 1978 a sizable number were imprisoned, placed under close surveillance (which restricted their activities), or forced to move underground. Since 1977, terrorist actions have been markedly reduced.

A new flurry of terrorist activity began after 6 September 1978, when Fidel Castro, in a press conference with foreign and Cuban emigré journalists, offered to engage in conversations with representatives of the exiled Cuban community, to discuss such issues as the liberation of political prisoners and the elimination of barriers to family visits.[20] The terrorists, realizing that such a dialogue would be the veritable end of counterrevolution, attempted to reassert their existence and prevent the increase of positive relationships between the emigrés and Cuba. At first, the traditional conservative leaders of the community (who feared a threat to their interests from these new developments) joined the heads of counterrevolutionary factions (the only category of people explicitly excluded by Fidel from the dialogue) in opposing the conversations.[21] Soon after, however, very broad sectors of the community moved to support the dialogue with Cuba, and the terrorists were forced to attack rather dubious objectives. Thus, on 21 October 1978, they bombed *El Diario–La Prensa*,[22] the major Spanish-language newspaper in New York City, one that had never been characterized by radicalism. The response of the community to such actions has been increasingly negative, and the terrorists more and more are finding themselves in isolation.

INCREASED PLURALISM

There has always been political heterogeneity in the exile community. For example, in the 1960–1964 period the very conservative *Batistianos* favored a return to the *status quo ante,* the prerevolutionary republic; the mostly liberal *reformistas,* such as the members of the Movimiento de Recuperación Revolucionaria, argued that the revolution was necessary but it had been "betrayed"; and the radicals, such as those in the Movimiento Revolucionario del Pueblo (accused by other exiles of being *"fidelistas sin Fidel"*), advocated most of the socioeconomic policies of the revolution while opposing the revolutionary leadership.

However, this early ideological pluralism was obscured by strategic uniformity. All of the movements mentioned above, and others as well, were committed to the violent overthrow of the revolutionary government, and were welded together (at least for a time) in the Consejo Revolucionario. They argued not over the validity of the current government—all were united against it—but over the image of the prerevolutionary republic and the policies to be pursued after the government's fall.

The current kind of heterogeneity is different. The political spectrum, if not expanded, is at least denser; ideologies range from quasifascist (e.g., the Comandos Nacionalistas) to Marxist (the Juventud Cubana Socialista), with all kinds of positions in between. Moreover, the various groups are no longer united for the violent overthrow of the Cuban regime: while some remain committed to that action, others wish to return to Cuba to integrate themselves into the revolutionary process, and again there are many positions in between. Some organizations are concerned less with Cuba itself than with the needs of Cubans in the United States—for instance, the Cuban National Planning Council and the Spanish American League Against Discrimination. There are also groups that emphasize professional goals (the Colegio Médico) and cultural activities (the Centro Cultural Cubano de Nueva York).

EMERGENCE OF RADICAL MOVEMENTS AMONG THE YOUTH

Most Cuban youth, especially outside the areas of large Cuban concentration, are quietly becoming assimilated into U.S. society. However, significant numbers have questioned the assimilation option and are searching for their national roots and a role as political actors.

Toward the political right is the organization known as Abdala, which rejects (at least verbally) the values of the U.S. consumer society. Abdala has adopted the militant style of U.S. youth movements of the 1960s in its drive for violent counterrevolution. Though its influence has diminished since 1972, it has managed to use Cuban clubs in universities and colleges to spread its views, and in the middle 1970s attempted to organize these clubs into a Federación Estudiantil Universitaria Cubana (Cuban University Students' Federation). These organizational attempts failed, but Abdala still controls many important Cuban clubs and associations in colleges and universities of the northeast, particularly in New Jersey and Washington. In recent years Abdala members have begun to define themselves as social democrats, perhaps reflecting a desire to be more effective among a Cuban youth increasingly more educated and exposed to liberal (and even radical) thought in U.S. colleges and universities.

An example of a radical youth group on the political left is the Juventud Cubana Socialista (Cuban Socialist Youth), which was active between 1970 and 1972. Although they were never well organized, the members collaborated with such U.S. radical organizations as the Venceremos Brigade and marched in New York in 1970 in favor of Puerto Rican independence.[23]

The most significant recent development is the proliferation of magazines representing various points of view from the center to the left of the political spectrum. The veteran of left-of-center Cuban youth publications was *Nueva Generación*, founded in Miami in the late 1960s and published in New York until 1974. *Areíto*, which published its first issue in New York in the spring of 1974, has become the rallying point for progressive U.S. Cubans and a source of controversy within the *colonias*. Partly in response to it, several magazines emerged in 1974 and 1975, ranging from *Cuba Va!* (Miami), which offered a supposedly Marxist critique of the revolution, to *Krisis* (Miami), which had what might be called a Solzhenitsyn wavelength. In general these two magazines emphasized libertarian issues, particularly freedom of artistic and intellectual expression in Cuba. *Joven Cuba*, a progressive magazine published in Boston by young Cubans from the northeastern *colonias*, placed a unique emphasis on the struggles of Hispanic minorities in the

United States. The latter magazines have tended to be irregular and short-lived. *Areíto*, however, has proven durable and highly influential. It is now entering its sixth year of publication.

Until recently the scholarly discussion among Cuban emigrés was seldom free from obvious bias. But a new type of emigré scholar has emerged, willing to study the transformations within Cuba with a spirit of openness. While these scholars range widely in their ideological positions, they share a serious and studious approach to the Cuban Revolution. See, for example, the works of Mesa-Lago (1971, 1975), Bonachea and Valdés (1969, 1972a, 1972b), Casal (1975, 1976), and Domínguez (1978). Many of these scholars have been brought together by the Instituto de Estudios Cubanos (Institute of Cuban Studies) in Washington, D.C. The Institute holds biennial conventions, regional meetings, and specialized seminars, and publishes a bimonthly bulletin, *Reunión*. Another magazine that publishes articles by these young (and not so young) scholars is *Cuban Studies/Estudios Cubanos*, issued by the Center for Latin American Studies at the University of Pittsburgh.

The Cuban Colonias and U.S. Policies

Cubans represent a small minority on the U.S. political scene and until recently had not even become U.S. citizens in sufficient numbers to be a significant force at election time. It is not surprising, then, that they have lacked political clout. Wong (1973) reported a Republican preference in 46 percent of the respondents in his Miami sample, compared to 34 percent with a Democratic preference and 20 percent with no preference; however, only 10 percent of his respondents were U.S. citizens.

In the future Cubans can be expected to have an increasingly important role in local politics in areas such as Miami and West New York–Union City. Salter and Mings (1972), who studied the potential impact of Cubans on voting patterns in metropolitan Miami, concluded that as their numbers and political activity increased, Cubans would provoke a shift toward generally anti-Communist and conservative candidates. However, Cuban progress even in Miami has been slow. Despite the fact that the federal government, through the Cuban Refugee Program, has spent more than $130 million on the Dade County public school system since 1960, it was not until 1973 that the school board had a Cuban member—A. Durán, former-president Prio's son-in-law.

At the national level Cuban influence has also been slow to increase. Even within the Cuban Refugee Program, the federal program designed especially to deal with Cubans in the United States, there were no Cubans at policy-making levels until late 1975, when R. Nuñez Portuondo was appointed to head the program.[24] The few Cuban successes came mainly through special channels: it seems, for instance, that the late Manolo Giberga, through the president's Committee for Spanish Speaking Americans, helped to effect the changes in U.S. immigration policy that opened the door to Cubans in Spain. Within the last several years, however, Cuban political activism within the U.S. political system has risen markedly. Recently some organizations, such as the Cuban National Planning Council, have tried specifically to influence U.S. domestic policies toward Cubans, promoting awareness of Cuban needs and seeking a share for Cubans in the federal gravy train. Occasional groups have also arisen at election time in support of various presidential hopefuls. The election of President Carter boosted the Democratic Party among Cubans and the political careers of a number of Cuban Democrats. Thus, A. Durán became the highest-ranking Democrat in the state of Florida; a small but significant number of Cubans entered the federal government; and a Washington-based National Coalition of Cuban Americans developed, to foster Cubans' political participation and insure an adequate flow of federal dollars to programs in the Cuban community. These Cubans have provided some input to the federal government on Cuban issues.

With respect to U.S. policies toward Cuba, the Cuban exiles have been manipulated more often than they have been manipulators. Except when their interests coincided with U.S. policies, they have had little impact. This is not an unusual state of affairs for an immigrant group. Although Moynihan (1975) has stressed the importance of ethnic groups, Cohen's study of State Department officials (1973) suggested that contacts with ethnic groups were used primarily for muting or manipulating ethnic demands. Garrett (1976) concluded that ethnic lobbying on American policy toward east-central Europe followed Cohen's pattern, and Hilsman (1971) suggested that the impact of specialized groups on foreign policy was rather limited.

Government responsiveness to such groups seems to be directly related to how well they can demonstrate that a certain policy furthers or damages their interests. For most internal policy decisions this task is relatively easy, and interest groups therefore have a strong input in domestic policy formulation. On the other hand, with the exception of tariffs and other special issues, it is hard to demonstrate the direct relationship of a certain foreign policy decision to the particular interests of a group.

Chittick (1970) has argued that for an interest group to be effective in its lobbying efforts it must be national in scope, it must have access to media for the dissemination of information, and it must be considered "responsible" in its approach by government officials and members of other organizations. Cuban exile groups involved in attempting to alter U.S. policies toward Cuba have been lacking in these prerequisite conditions. Only since 1976 have groups emerged which seem to have better lobbying chances. Cubans are gradually becoming more savvy in terms of the workings of the U.S. political system. A recently organized group, the Cuban American Committee for the Normalization of Relations, has become increasingly effective in reaching congressmen, members of the national media, and other decision makers. It seems likely, then, that the emigrés' influence on U.S. policies toward Cuba will grow.

With regard to the potential impact of the Cuban communities upon the delicate process of resumption of commercial and diplomatic ties between Cuba and the United States, a few tentative generalizations can be advanced.

1. Faced with the prospect of a change in U.S. policy toward Cuba, the most conservative elements in the Cuban community have reacted with verbal and physical terrorism which only stresses their powerlessness as political agents. Furthermore, the Cuban community is not monolithic now (if it ever was) and there are strong suggestions—the dominant mass media in the exile *colonias* notwithstanding—that most Cubans in the United States would favor re-establishment of U.S.-Cuban ties or at least would not oppose it.

A 1975 survey conducted by two Florida International University students and published in *The Miami Herald* (29 December 1975) indicated that 53 percent of Miami Cubans opposed the resumption of diplomatic relations between the United States and Cuba; conversely, 47 percent did not oppose it. Since little information was given about the methodology of the survey, we cannot judge the representativeness of the sample. But the figures represent a significant growth of pro-resumption opinion compared to an earlier *Herald* survey. Furthermore, if one takes into consideration that Miami Cubans are probably more conservative on this and other issues than Cubans in other *colonias*, it is safe to estimate that most Cubans in the United States today do not oppose U.S.-Cuban ties. Significant age and sex differentials were also revealed in the Miami survey. Men opposed resumption of ties more than women; and opposition to resumption increased very clearly with age: among the 16–25 age group only 27 percent opposed ties, and

in the 26–39 age bracket only 49 percent did. The greatest opposition
was found in the over-60 group, in which 84 percent opposed resumption of ties. The influence and weight of the older groups are naturally
dwindling. And it must be pointed out that even among those opposed
to resumption of ties, a sizable percentage (28.9 percent) said they
would visit Cuba if their return to the United States were guaranteed.
For the total sample, the percentage that would visit Cuba was 49.5.
These figures suggest the strength of nostalgia among exiles of diverse
political orientations.

In recent years, several groups have emerged within the Cuban
colonias which advocate an end to the blockade and the resumption
of diplomatic relations between Cuba and the United States. The magazine *Areito*, since its maiden issue (April 1974), has consistently taken
such a position in its editorials. *Areito*, and other groups on the left of
the exile political spectrum, stress the bankruptcy of U.S. policies
toward Cuba, the consolidation and institutionalization of the Cuban
revolution, the advantages of resumption of relationships for the Cuban people, including the Cuban *colonias* in the United States, and the
need for the U.S. to deal with Cuba as an equal, sovereign state (a goal
incompatible with the maintenance of the blockade). In 1974, a group
of Cubans, mostly Protestant pastors and faithful of various denomina-
tions, organized the Cristianos Cubanos pro Justicia y Libertad (Cuban
Christians for Justice and Freedom). This group, starting from an analysis of the "new situation" which stressed the stability of the Cuban
revolutionary regime, its process of institutionalization, and its growing
international recognition within the overall context of détente, has
been actively engaged in promoting the elimination of the blockade
and the resumption of diplomatic ties between Cuba and the United
States. It published an advertisement in *The New York Times* (13
April 1975); two of its leaders testified in front of subcommittees of the
Committee on International Relations of the U.S. House of Representatives (26 June 1975); it publishes a bulletin promoting its views
(*Nuevos Horizontes*, Tampa, Florida); and it organized a National
Consultation on the Cuban situation, which took place in New York
City in March 1976 with the participation of individuals from various
organizations within the center-left segment of the exile political spectrum. The Consultation issued a declaration advocating the lifting of
the blockade and the resumption of diplomatic ties between Cuba and
the United States—despite the poor climate for such moves created by
election-year campaigning and the reactions to Cuban involvement in
Angola.

Other religious groups have also been active in the movement
toward resumption of relations and family reunification. In Hialeah,

Florida, a church directed by Rev. Manuel Espinosa has been energetically recruiting Cubans, mostly from the working class, who want to visit relatives on the island. Its membership rolls have lately grown dramatically, and toward the end of 1978 had surpassed the 2,000 mark. Rev. Espinosa and his church have been actively lobbying in Washington for a different Cuban policy and urging Havana (mostly through the Cuban consulate in Jamaica) toward an open policy on family visits. The church publishes a magazine named *Wahini*.

One of the most important new organizations is the Brigade Antonio Maceo, composed of men and women who left Cuba as minors because of parental decision. Their first group (55 persons) travelled to Cuba during December 1977 and engaged in construction work there. They had extensive contacts with officials at different levels and undertook a tour of the island. Their impact upon the emigré community, as well as upon the Cuban people and revolutionary leadership, cannot be stressed enough.[25]

This is only the tip of the iceberg. Dozens of smaller organizations and groups have emerged, particularly in response to Fidel Castro's invitation to dialogue on 6 September 1978. Besides isolating and marginalizing the terrorists, as pointed out earlier, the new Cuban policy is bound to have far-reaching consequences, further decreasing counter-revolutionary activities and fostering the shift of the community's median opinion toward peaceful coexistence, resumption of diplomatic relations between Cuba and the U.S., and acceptance of the Cuban regime. Furthermore, the new dialogue will create a significant traffic to the island (given the increased family and tourist visits), and this will have important effects in the immediate future.

2. Even if the Cuban communities are not capable by themselves of generating a change in U.S. policies, they have acted in the past as a contributing factor to deter such a change. Until 1975, the U.S. had, with tactical variations throughout the years, a fairly consistent policy of hostility toward Cuba. The political costs of this policy had already been paid. To change the policy, the risk (and possible costs) of the new course had to be considered. The presumed monolithic opposition of the Cuban community added to these anticipated costs and to the likelihood of the use of the "Cuban issue" by the U.S. right.

In spite of such risks and the negative reaction of the Carter administration to Cuba's African activities, there have been significant changes since 1975. These changes stand in dialectical relationship to attitudes in the Cuban community. As the attitudes of U.S. Cubans have become more heterogeneous, it has been less possible to use the Cuban community as a deterrent or delaying element in U.S. policy analyses. In turn, as the U.S. has changed its positions (in spite of the ups and downs of the last several years), the Cuban community has increasingly perceived normalization as inevitable and desirable.

President Castro's position in his press conference of September 1978 has served to defuse many of the "human rights" issues of primary concern to the Cuban community—issues, such as the liberation of political prisoners and the easing of travel restrictions, that could have been brought to bear on U.S.-Cuban negotiations. Thus, the probability that the emigré communities in the U.S. could be used as a pressure group against Cuba in the eventual negotiating process has been sharply reduced. As a matter of fact, it seems that the Cuban community has been neutralized in terms of its potential negative impact (for Cuba) upon the negotiations. At the same time, it can be safely predicted that more and more U.S. Cubans will press for normalization of relations, resumption of regular flights, and so on.

3. As the United States and Cuba move toward normalization of relations, an increase in the violent activities of groups toward the extreme right of the exile political spectrum can be expected. These groups will probably attempt to secure in the future, as they have in the past, support from those regimes in the hemisphere that feel most threatened by the Cuban revolutionary regime, such as the Chilean junta. The rightist Cuban groups will try to hinder the expression of the wide range of positions that now exists within the Cuban community. Their dangerousness and, at the very least, their nuisance value cannot be overemphasized. However, in this author's opinion, these groups are manifestations of powerlessness and despair and are not likely to have a substantial impact on policy formulation or the bargaining process.

The strategy of those right and center groups opposed to the normalization of relations is likely to be one of emphasizing the dangerousness of Cuba's position of solidarity with liberation movements throughout the world and of exaggerating the importance of this to U.S. national security. In this respect, they would be following the lead of U.S. hardliners.

4. Recent events, such as the dialogue proposed by President Castro, have provoked monumental changes in the emigré community's leadership structure, thus restricting even further the influence of the far right. The process began in the early seventies as many new "leaders" emerged: people involved in local community affairs or professional and cultural activities. Generally the late seventies have witnessed the emergence of organized local and national Cuban American political groups with their corresponding crop of leaders. In particular, the months since President Castro's press conference have seen the ascent to prominence of a group of men and women who are participating in

the efforts to negotiate with the Cuban regime. The old organized groups within the community have been placed under considerable strain, and their refusal to engage in the dialogue has only accelerated their demise as active factors in the life of the *colonias*.

5. As the pluralization of the Cuban *colonias* has progressed, and particularly as a new generation of young Cubans interested in re-evaluating the Cuban revolutionary process has emerged, the Cuban government has begun to reconsider its view of the emigration. A hindrance to this process seems to have been the fact that the Cuban exiles, in an overwhelming proportion, reside in the United States. Thus the Cuban government has considered that any shift in its policies toward exiles would be looked upon by the U.S. government as a signal to the United States. In spite of these difficulties, major changes have occurred in the Cuban approach to the emigré *colonias* since 1972:

(a) The subtle change in labels. Exiles are now frequently called *emigrados* (emigrés) rather than *gusanos* (worms), the formerly ubiquitous term used by the Cuban leaders and the Cuban mass media. In his September 1978 press conference, President Castro addressed the emigré *colonias* as *la comunidad* (the community) and criticized the former use of "unjust generic terms" such as *gusanos*.

(b) The fact that the Cuban constitution of 1975 clearly recognizes the emigrés as Cuban citizens (with the exception of those who may be engaged in activities against the Cuban state and others whose citizenship has been explicitly revoked).

(c) The opening of Cuba's doors to emigré visitors. A number of young exiles and Cuban academics were invited to visit Cuba on a limited and selective basis, beginning in 1973.[26] They were followed by the relatively large group (55 young people) of the Antonio Maceo Brigade in December 1977. A smaller group of Cuban youth from the Brigade visited the island during the Festival of Youth (summer 1978) as members of delegations from the United States, Puerto Rico, Mexico, Venezuela, and Spain. Also, a large group from the church of Rev. Espinosa in Hialeah visited relatives in Cuba during the fall of 1978.

Besides these special group visits, policy has changed to allow routine visits by Cubans who had left the island by 1958 and also by younger Cubans who became unwilling emigrés because of their parents' decisions.

Thus, the Cuban regime has developed differentiated responses to various individuals, groups, and sectors within the Cuban *colonias*—responses based on recognition of the heterogeneity of the *colonias*. Furthermore, the Cuban government has established a new policy of openness with respect to family visits and seems willing to consider other aspects of the family reunification question.[27]

All of these trends help to strengthen forces within the Cuban *colonias* favorable to the resumption of relations between Cuba and the United States. Cuba's image becomes more positive as thorny "human rights" issues are defused. Cuba is also likely to be strengthened economically by increased visits from U.S. Cubans, who can become a significant source of hard currency. One can surmise that these consequences of Cuba's recent attitude may not be altogether unintended.

Notes

1. In 1970 roughly 45 percent of all U.S. Cubans lived in the Miami area, and the percentage has probably increased since then.

2. A sizable bibliography on Cuban exiles has accumulated. For surveys of this literature, see Casal and Hernández (1975), Hernández (1974), and Prohías and Casal (1973).

3. The Cuban Refugee Program is the name given to the overall program developed by the federal government in response to the Cuban migration of the sixties. It has included a variety of elements, from student loans (nationwide) and retraining programs for professionals (held in various locations throughout the U.S.) to "impact" funds granted to the Dade County school system to offset the additional expenses caused by the Cuban influx. The Cuban Refugee Center, referred to on following pages, is the name given to the Miami office which actually processed most of the incoming refugees, provided services for the Miami settlers, coordinated the resettlement program, and so on.

4. Prohías and Casal also found wide regional variations in the Census's accuracy: for example, the underestimation for Florida was twice the national figure.

5. Priority was granted to relatives of persons already living in the United States: spouses, parents of unmarried children under the age of 21, and brothers and sisters under the age of 21 (Thomas 1967).

6. Cf. *Life*, 10 December 1971; "Our Latin Accent," a special supplement to *The Miami Herald*, 18 June 1971; and Susan Jacoby, "Miami Sí, Cuba No," *The New York Times Magazine*, 29 September 1974.

7. Cuban Refugee Program funds, although disbursed through the Department of Health, Education and Welfare, of which the CRP is an administrative dependency, have been appropriated, at different stages, under the 1954 Mutual Security Act, the Foreign Assistance Act of 1961, and the Migration and Refugee Assistance Act of 28 June 1962. In terms of U.S. foreign policies, the program acted as a lure to induce Cubans to emigrate and as an element in the campaign to discredit the Cuban revolution internationally; in terms of domestic policies, the program served to silence the potential or actual complaints from localities affected by the refugee influx—localities which refused to pay for what was fundamentally a foreign policy decision.

8. Although primarily designed to aid states and localities with its "impact funds," the refugee assistance program has at least in part directly aided emigrés.

9. *The Miami Herald*, 21 October 1975.

10. See the Appendix to the U.S. Budget for fiscal year 1974.

11. *The Miami Herald*, 21 October 1975.

12. Cf. Alford 1973:215–16; *Life*, 10 December 1971; *Cuba Resource Center Newsletter*, July 1972.

13. Torriente claimed to have a secret plan (the details of which were never revealed) to liberate Cuba. He spoke as if he had U.S. backing or connections. See *Nuestra Cuba* (a New Jersey tabloid), 31 January 1974, p. 6.

14. See *The Miami Herald*, 5 December 1975, for a chronology of bombings during this period.

15. *Ibid.*, 4 December 1975.

16. *Ibid.*, 8 October 1975.

17. *Ibid.*, 6 December 1975.

18. In *The New York Times* (14 December 1975), George Volsky reported that terrorist activities contributed to anti-Cuban sentiment in Miami.

19. For a discussion of connections between former or present mobsters and anti-Communist Cubans, U.S. politicians, and both Cuban and U.S. businessmen, see Sutton (1973).

20. For the complete text of Fidel Castro's press conference, see *Granma*, 8 September 1978.

21. See, for example, the *Diario de las Américas* (Miami), 19 September 1978, p. 22.

22. See *El Diario–La Prensa*, 23 October 1978, and following.

23. See the *Cuba Resource Center Newsletter*, July 1972, pp. 25–28, which reproduces a statement of the Cuban Socialist Youth that was widely circulated in the underground press.

24. *The Miami Herald*, 31 December 1975.

25. For a description of the Brigade and testimonies from the visitors, see *Areíto* 4, nos. 3–4 (Spring 1978).

26. For the impressions of Cuba of nine such travelers, see *Areíto* 2, nos. 2–3 (September–December 1975).

27. The situation is constantly changing as this is written in October 1978.

References

Alford, Harold J. 1973. *The Proud Peoples.* New York: New American Library.

Bonachea, Rolando E., and Valdés, Nelson P. 1969. *Che: Selected Works of Ernesto Guevara.* Cambridge, Mass.: M.I.T. Press.

———. 1972a. *Cuba in Revolution.* Garden City, N.Y.: Anchor Books.

——. 1972b. *Revolutionary Struggle: The Selected Works of Fidel Castro.* Cambridge, Mass.: M.I.T. Press.

Casal, L. 1975. On popular power: The organization of the Cuban state during the period of transition. *Latin American Perspectives* 2, no. 4 (supplement):78–88.

——. 1976. The Cuban Communist Party: "The best among the good." *Cuba Review* 6, no. 3 (September):23–30.

——, and Hernández, Andrés R. 1975. Cubans in the U.S.: A survey of the literature. *Cuban Studies/Estudios Cubanos* 5, no. 2 (July):25–51.

Chittick, William. 1970. *State Department, Press and Pressure Groups.* New York: Wiley Interscience.

Clark, Juan M. 1970. The Cuban escapees as possible factual indicators of Cuban social conditions. *Latinamericanist* 6, no. 1:1–4.

Cohen, Bernard C. 1973. *The Public's Impact on Foreign Policy.* Boston: Little, Brown.

Díaz, Guarioné. 1970. El proceso de pluralización del exilio cubano. *Nueva Generación* 3, no. 20 (November):16–27.

——. 1974. Despolitización y detente. *Nueva Generación* 4, no. 27 (June): 13–20.

Domínguez, Jorge. 1978. *Cuba: Order and Revolution.* Cambridge, Mass.: The Belknap Press of Harvard University Press.

Domínguez, Virginia. 1975. *From Neighbor to Stranger: The Dilemma of Caribbean Peoples in the United States.* New Haven: Antilles Research Program, Yale University.

Fagen, Richard R., Brody, Richard A., and O'Leary, Thomas J. 1968. *Cubans in Exile: Disaffection and the Revolution.* Stanford: Stanford University Press.

Garrett, Stephen A. 1976. The ties that bind: Immigrant influence on American foreign policy toward Eastern Europe. Paper presented at the 17th Annual Convention of the International Studies Association, Toronto, February.

Hernández, Andrés R., ed. 1974. *The Cuban Minority in the U.S.: Final Report on Need Identification and Program Evaluation.* Washington, D.C.: Cuban National Planning Council.

Hilsman, Roger. 1971. *The Politics of Policy-Making in Defense and Foreign Affairs.* New York: Harper and Row.

Mesa-Lago, Carmelo. 1971. *Revolutionary Change in Cuba.* Pittsburgh: University of Pittsburgh Press.

——. 1975. *Cuba in the 1970s: Pragmatism and Institutionalization.* Albuquerque: University of New Mexico Press.

Moncarz, Raul. 1969. *A Study of the Effect of Environmental Change on Human Capital Among Selected Skilled Cubans.* Document PB 186 396. Washington, D.C.: Clearinghouse for Federal Scientific and Technical Information, U.S. Department of Commerce.

Moynihan, Daniel P., ed. 1975. *Ethnicity: Theory and Experience.* Cambridge, Mass.: Harvard University Press.

Portes, Alejandro. 1969. Dilemmas of a golden exile: Integration of Cuban refugee families in Milwaukee. *American Sociological Review* 34 (August): 505–18.

Prohías, Rafael. 1967. The Cuban exile community in Indianapolis: A study in accommodation. Unpublished semester report, Indiana University, January. Abbreviated version published in Spanish as: Cubanos en Indianápolis: Un ejemplo de acomodación. *Nueva Generación* 2, no. 14 (September–October 1967):7–8.

———, and Casal, Lourdes. 1973. *The Cuban Minority in the U.S.: Preliminary Report on Need Identification and Program Evaluation.* Boca Raton, Fla.: Florida Atlantic University.

Rogg, Eleanor H. 1970. The occupational adjustment of Cuban refugees in the West New York, New Jersey, area. Unpublished Ph.D. dissertation, Fordham University. Later revised and published as *The Assimilation of Cuban Exiles: The Role of Community and Class.* New York: Aberdeen, 1974.

Salter, Paul S., and Mings, Robert C. 1972. The projected impact of Cuban settlement on voting patterns in metropolitan Miami, Florida. *The Professional Geographer* 24:123–31.

Sutton, Horace. 1973. The curious intrigues of Cuban Miami. *Saturday Review World* 1, no. 1 (11 September):24–31.

Thomas, John F. 1967. Cuban refugees in the U.S. *International Migration Review* 1, no. 2 (Spring):46–57.

University of Miami, Center for International Studies, Research Institute for Cuba and the Caribbean. 1967. *The Cuban Immigration 1959–1966 and Its Impact on Miami, Dade County, Florida.* Coral Gables: University of Miami.

U.S. Department of Commerce, Bureau of the Census. 1972. *Selected Characteristics of Persons and Families of Mexican, Puerto Rican and Other Spanish Origin, March 1972.* Current Population Reports, Population Characteristics, series P-20, no. 238 (July).

U.S. Department of Labor. 1973. *Manpower Report of the President.* Washington, D.C.: Government Printing Office.

Walsh, Msgr. Bryan O. 1971. Cuban refugee children. *Journal of Inter-American Studies and World Affairs* 13:378–414.

Wenk, M. G. 1968. Adjustment and assimilation: The Cuban refugee experience. *International Migration Review* 3, no. 1 (Fall):38–49.

Wong, Francisco. 1973. Political orientations and participation of Cuban migrants: A preliminary analysis. Paper presented at the Annual Convention of the American Political Science Association, New Orleans, September.

Cuban Ideology and Nationhood: Their Meaning in the Americas

NITA ROUS MANITZAS

> Communism has . . . provided a powerful vehicle of modernization where other alternatives failed. / Giorgio Borsa, 1964

> This is what Cuba symbolized for the Americas. A hope and an alternative. / Fernando Henrique Cardoso, 1973

> . . . the Cubans are on the verge of making their system work. / Staff Report, U.S. Senate, 1974

To understand the evolving pattern of Cuba's relations in the hemisphere, the ideological pulls on its external behavior, the variety of policy options the island may follow, and the possible responses from other American states, is a complex exercise. The variables are multiple, and they do not sit still for us. The controlled conditions of the hard-science laboratory do not exist for policy makers and social scientists. Not only is the Cuban system changing and maturing internally, but the environment in which Cuba acts out its external role also is fluid. The diagnoses that appear so persuasive on paper at a given time may well prove invalid under live, shifting circumstances. The course of human affairs is neither predetermined nor unilinear. And individual actors, whether national leaders or common assassins, can make choices that will alter historical trajectories.

In such a complex and changeful universe, political assessments are hazardous enterprises. Nevertheless, it behooves us to attempt to give some explanatory order to the hectic behavior of human beings and nations, to determine what is generalizable and what is unique in

137

a given historical situation, and to distinguish between those phenomena that have only surface significance and those that form consistent patterns. No one can predict the future; but empirical data, properly ordered, can at least help us to gauge probabilities. The task requires dispassion and historical perspective. After nearly two decades of the Revolution in power, both should be possible in considering the Cuban case.

A first step in the process is to locate Cuba inside an appropriate category of analysis. Thanks to the myopia of the Cold War, which saw the world in Manichean absolutes, those countries that have "gone Communist" since World War II have been automatically banished from North American development literature. While economic and social indicators may place them squarely in the ranks of the so-called less-developed nations, they are outside the pale of development theory. In this Cold War wonderland, Argentina is an underdeveloped country; Albania is not. Both in U.S. academia and in the State Department, member nations of the socialist camp are consigned willy-nilly to the intellectual care of Sovietologists, specialists in comparative Communism, and "area" experts. The fact that these countries may be grappling with the same structural, technological, and economic problems that afflict all less-developed states is not deemed relevant. Similarly, the solutions they may devise also are irrelevant for development theorists. When Fidel Castro declared himself a Marxist-Leninist in December 1961, Cuba was not only drummed out of the Organization of American States, but out of the mainstream of development literature as well.

While there is still much emotional rhetoric about the island and its ties to the Soviet Union, there is a growing perception among many North Americans and Latin Americans that Cuba represents something more than a typical Soviet client state. Despite its current links to the Kremlin and its espousal of Marxism-Leninism as a formal ideology, Cuba cannot be conceptually fit—except by prodigious and astigmatic effort—into the standard mold of an East European people's republic. It does not share in the centuries-old tradition of pan-Slavism. It holds no subconscious residues from the Byzantine Empire, the Ottoman invaders, or the Hapsburg dynasty. Nor does it share in the accumulated experience of Great Russian expansionism, world wars, Stalinist purges, Nazi occupation, the subsequent incursions of the Red Army, or a host of other collective memories that knit Eastern Europe in special fashion to the Soviet Union. There are no common language roots. There are no common cultural traditions. And, perhaps most important, there are some six thousand miles of geographical distance separating Cuba from the Soviet frontier. To classify Cuba simply as another Soviet satellite, one that happens to be floating ninety miles off the U.S. coast, may have a certain logic in the Pentagon; but it makes no sense in social science or anywhere else. It certainly does not reflect the image that significant numbers of Latin Americans have of Cuba and, hence, the ways in which the American states are likely to relate to the island in the future.

By its own definition and by standard economic indicators, Cuba is a card-carrying member of that group of nations commonly classified as "less developed." As Fidel himself remarked in his speech of 30 December 1973, "We're a small, underdeveloped country, with limited natural resources and no energy sources" (*Granma Weekly Review*, 13 January 1974). This has been a recurring theme in the pronouncements of the Cuban leadership since the onset of their revolution. The sense of "underdevelopment" imparts a special texture to Cuba's national ideology and to Cuba's particular, Caribbean adaptation of Marxism-Leninism. In the international arena, it also colors the island's pattern of relations and alliances. Despite its alignment with the Soviet Union, it is clear from even a cursory analysis of Cuban speeches and publications that the island's basic self-image is one of membership in the so-called Third World. Inside the socialist camp, although the Cubans treat their COMECON partners with considerable public cordiality (which was not always the case some years ago), their deeper affinities lie outside the European continent. Their affective ties have been consistently closer to such socialist countries as North Vietnam and, in its time, to Salvador Allende's Chile.

Beyond the socialist bloc, as well, Cuba has persistently emphasized its allegiance to and identification with the more disadvantaged members of the global community. The ideological stance of Cuba's leaders may often bring them into conflict and confrontation with specific governments of the Third World, but their explicit identity of interests with the mass of the population in the less developed regions of Asia, Africa, and Latin America is a Cuban constant. It is not merely rhetorical posturing, reserved for public display at gatherings of the nonaligned countries and other international forums. On the contrary, Cuba's solidarity with the less developed tier of nations is an intrinsic element in the political socialization of every Cuban schoolchild, and service in such remote places as Algeria, the Congo, and more recently Angola and Ethiopia has been a Cuban calling since the early 1960s. It represents the projection onto the international stage of one of the fundamental strands of Cuba's internal, national ideology.

If Cuba's self-image is rooted in the Third World, within that broad category there is a special identification and intimacy with a particular subset of developing nations. Cuba is a Latin American country. And it shares with the rest of Latin America common ties of language, colonial experience, the wash of Western-Iberian-Catholic culture, and, in this century, continuing exposure to the weight and influence of the United States. (If anything, these characteristics were more pronounced in Cuba than anywhere else in the hemisphere. Spanish colonial rule persisted in Cuba for three-quarters of a century after the other Latin American republics had achieved their independence. Afterwards, until the onset of Fidel's Revolution, nowhere was the U.S. presence so direct or pervasive—culturally, politically, and economically—as it was in Cuba.) Whatever the subsequent permutations of Cuba's relations with its sister republics, the sense of common identity with the rest of Latin America remains. José Martí, the intellectual apostle of Cuba's independence from Spain, shared in the Bolivarian vision of a united Latin America. His repeated invocation of *nuestra América* has always been a standard part of the vocabulary of Cuba's new revolutionary leaders.

Even at the height of the quarantine, when all Latin American countries but Mexico had severed their formal ties with Cuba, the island maintained its sense of identification with the hemisphere. Conversely, even though diplomatic connections were cut, subgroups of Latin Americans—revolutionaries, intellectuals, and members of particular political parties—continued to travel to Cuba, some to visit briefly and some to work with the Revolution. These voyagers were nonofficial, mostly dissident in the prevailing Latin American climate, and anti-Establishment. They served to keep Cuba involved with a particular subculture in the hemisphere, an involvement that reached both its zenith and its nadir in 1967 with Che Guevara's unfruitful expedition into Bolivia.

In that era, Cuban ideology and the Cuban national model had mostly symbolic meaning in the Americas—of liberating revolution for some, and of hemispheric subversion for others, depending on the interests and viewpoint of the observer. Inside Cuba, the Revolution was still fluid, proceeding in apparently fitful and unpredictable directions. The economy was unsettled and, at times, bordered on the chaotic, leading friends and critics alike to predict imminent disaster. The institutional definition of Cuba's political order was as yet unclear. Cuba's survival in the face of unremitting pressure from its giant northern neighbor, its support for revolutionary movements in the hemisphere, and its emphasis on an egalitarian social order might have struck responsive chords with many Latin Americans; but the actual internal workings of the Cuban system and the potential significance of Cuba as an alternative model of national development were little understood or heeded.

That situation, and the appreciation of Cuba's meaning in the hemisphere, are changing. The reasons, as well as the possible consequences, are multiple, reflecting both the internal evolution of the Cuban system and the shifting conditions elsewhere in the Americas. In the late 1970s, Cuba can no longer be dismissed as an enclave of bearded rebels in battle dress thumbing their noses at the established rules of national decorum and development. On the contrary, the island must be taken seriously as a modernizing, functioning nation-state. Cuba's economic experiment, widely regarded some years ago as a peculiar aberration, has yielded an economic order that appears to be operating productively and more equitably than most of the more traditional economies of the Third World. Cuba's political system, which seemed to run *por la libre* under the capricious direction of a single charismatic leader, has acquired institutional process and procedures. The first congress of the Communist Party took place in December 1975. A new constitution was enacted in 1976. And, the same year, electoral politics were reinstituted—albeit with controls and conditions—for representative bodies at the municipal, provincial, and national levels of administration. Meanwhile, with diplomatic finesse, Cuba is re-entering the inter-American network and developing commercial relations world-wide. In sum, the revolutionary order has consolidated and matured; and, in any comparative ranking of Third World countries, the system is working well. This internal maturation obviously influences Cuba's comportment on the international stage. It will also affect the ways in which other countries come to regard Cuba and to assess the special developmental trajectory that Cuba has pursued.

The other side of the equation, of course, is the changing ambiance surrounding Cuba in the hemisphere. The international environment has shifted dramatically since 1959, in ways that were not necessarily anticipated when Fidel Castro and his rebel army first descended from the Sierra Maestra. The birth of OPEC, the growing coalition of non-aligned countries across the Third World, Soviet-U.S. détente, and a series of systemic jolts in the world economic order are only a few of the new realities that now affect the interplay among nation-states. Cuba's relations in the Americas, and the meaning with which the Cuban model is imbued in the hemisphere, will obviously be determined not solely by Cuba's own actions and policies, but also by the varied and changing conditions in other American states.

The New Inter-American Setting

In the last two decades, the environment in the Americas has undergone a series of radical alterations. In the early 1960s, the euphoria of John F. Kennedy's Camelot was infectious. It found a specially receptive audience in Latin America, where a goodly number of dictatorial regimes had recently come crashing down. In what was then happily called the "free world," it was thought that there were no problems that could not be solved by reasonable people using adequate technique, know-how, and sophisticated computer hardware. Ideology was supposedly dead, or at least irrelevant. The tool of the future was systems management: value-free, neutrally beneficial, and universally applicable in all geographical and cultural settings. Development was an attainable goal, if there were only sufficient will, planning, and entrepreneurial spirit. The United Nations, caught up in the general enthusiasm, was moved to bestow on the 1960s the title of the "First Development Decade." In the United States and elsewhere, national elites and common citizens were seduced by W. W. Rostow's neat vision of a world in which all countries, one after another, would march down the selfsame path to "takeoff." The watchwords were evolution, incremental reform, and above all economic growth. From this combination, it was supposed, all other good would flow—educational opportunity, social mobility, and political openness. Once GNP was healthily expanding, the other accoutrements of a modern, democratic nation-state would necessarily follow. In this felicitous scenario, revolutions were ruled out, since they would only interfere with orderly economic advance. Marxian ideology was simply a nasty doctrine peddled by the Soviet Union. Under no circumstances could socialism be seriously considered as a developmental alternative. Fidel's experiment was doomed to early failure, while the rest of the Americas, with U.S. technical aid and private capital investment, would ineluctably progress.

The optimism and confidence of that era are gone. The returns from the "First Development Decade" have been tallied, and they are dismal. The absolute number of the world's inhabitants who live below the minimal level of human decency has increased, not declined. Even where there has been a supposed "economic miracle," as in Brazil, it seems to have been accompanied by greater social inequalities, higher concentrations of wealth, and more political repression than before. The structural problems of underdevelopment have proved more profound and persistent than originally forecast. The oil-rich countries may be suddenly awash in new petrodollars, but the rest of the Third World is falling further and further behind. Meanwhile, the so-called developed world has learned, to its surprise, that even industrially advanced nations are not immune to inflation, economic stagnation, unemployment, class and ethnic conflicts, and other maladies that were thought to be the defining attributes of underdevelopment.

There is a new sense of unease in international circles, of problems that defy ready solution. If the threat of nuclear war between the two superpowers has receded, the possibility of localized conflicts, international terrorism, and civic violence inside nations seems to be escalating. Among the poorer countries, there is a growing conviction that the formulas and advice offered to them by their more affluent neighbors are neither so beneficial nor so altruistic as was once supposed. It is not only that the growth models prescribed as universally applicable and efficacious have proved wanting in practice. It also is the case that such spectacles as the Vietnam War, economic sanctions and other incursions into the affairs of Third World nations, and the open support of the United States for patently repressive governments have served to erode much of the earlier confidence in the ethical authority and good intentions of Western democratic capitalism. The Carter administration's new emphasis on human rights may allay some of the accumulated doubt and distrust, but a strong residue of skepticism necessarily will remain.

Throughout the Americas, in sum, the panorama has changed profoundly since John F. Kennedy first proposed the Alliance for Progress as an alternative and an antidote to Fidel's brand of revolution. The Alliance itself, of course, has long since passed into historical oblivion. The quantitative goals that were happily projected were never attained by most Latin American states. Qualitatively, the doctrine of an *abrazo* for democratic governments and a cool handshake for dictators did not survive even to mid-decade. Successive interventions in the internal affairs of Western Hemisphere nations—whether overt, as in the landing of marines in Santo Domingo, or covert, as in the destabilization of the Allende government in Chile—led Latin Americans to doubt whether the United States was indeed a benign and disinterested partner. The activities of multinational corporations, control over natural resources, and the terms of trade for raw materials and semi-finished goods have become major points of friction between Latin American governments and the United States. Most Latin American leaders were irritated by what they took to be Mr. Kissinger's cavalier policy toward their region; and they are dissatisfied now with the relative neglect of the Carter administration, as they perceive it. As a result, many Latin American countries have shown themselves progressively less inclined to follow the North American lead, whether in trade relations, diplomacy, or the continued quarantine of Cuba. The creation in 1975 of the Latin American Economic System (SELA), conspicuously excluding the United States, was an indicative symptom of the changing climate.

The internal political configuration of Latin America also has been shifting. Among the more notable occurrences is the proliferation of military regimes in the region. The number of countries that enjoy even partially consensual forms of government has been inexorably shrinking. The new generation of the Latin American military, moreover, are more professional and cohesive than their predecessors. They bear little resemblance to Batista's motley soldiery, as Latin American guerrillas have painfully learned. Their coups are not comic operas. And their institutional role is expanding well beyond the traditional limits of national security and internal public order into the more complex realm of socioeconomic control and economic policy. They no longer make their *golpes* to pave the way for new civilian elections and governors. Where the military have now taken power, they see themselves as the purveyors of national ideology; in the economic arena, they are the guardians of the development process; and in the social sphere they use their monopoly of force to restrain mobility, dissent, and popular participation in ways that will permit the economic engine to function independently of the needs and desires of the mass of civilian citizenry.

One should be careful not to carry the generalizations too far, of course. Apart from the uniform and the anti-Marxist rhetoric, there is more difference than commonality between a General Geisel, managing a mammoth technocratic bureaucracy in Brazil, and a Somoza, presiding over a little patrimonial fiefdom in Nicaragua. Pinochet's style of governance in Chile is far removed from the relatively benign, relatively populist performance of the military authorities in neighboring Peru. Indeed, a significant feature of contemporary Latin America is the diversity of institutional accommodations, whether one speaks of those few countries that still maintain the outward forms of democracy or those that have adopted authoritarian regimens. Nationalism and "developmentalism" may now be the common ideological constants in most Latin American states, but they come packaged in a wide variety of ways. At one end of the spectrum are small, largely rural, patrimonial regimes governed by personalistic *caudillos*. At the other extreme, Latin America may be on the way to having its first full-scale, fascistic, totalitarian states, with all the electronic trimmings. In between, the gamut runs from traditional, civilian oligarchies through liberal, middle-class democracies to technocratic-authoritarian systems containing varying mixes of corporativism.* There are no "pure types" in this

---

*For an interesting and more orderly typology of governmental situations in Latin America, see Silvert (1975).

array, and none of these institutional situations is static: they are in a constant state of evolution and "becoming."

The variety of governmental situations and their fluid state suggest the possibility of considerable diversity among Latin American nations in their formal responses and reactions to Cuba. Chile, Paraguay, and Uruguay, so long as their current authorities remain in power, are likely to continue treating Cuba as a sinister presence in the hemisphere which, if it cannot be exorcised, should at least be segregated from everyone else. Other countries, such as Panama and Peru, while they may not share Cuba's ideological position, may well find mutualities of interest with the island on particular issues, especially those that involve dispute and confrontation with the United States. A third tier of countries may find the establishment of outwardly cordial relations with Cuba a useful way of placating internal leftist groups without necessarily granting them any significant domestic concessions. And, in yet another set of cases, certain Latin American governments may come to regard Cuba, with its improved economic prospects, as a potentially attractive trading partner. In other words, the pattern of governmental responses to Cuba's re-entry into the inter-American network will most likely be varied, leaving room for substantial "play" in the policy options that Cuba may exercise at the diplomatic level.

Formal diplomacy, however, is only the tip of the iceberg. It does not by any means exhaust the range of possible relations that Cuba may establish in the hemisphere or the meanings that the Cuban model may come to assume for different subnational groups. However authoritatively Latin American governments may speak in the international arena, their official powers and prerogatives do not necessarily mean that they represent anything approximating a national consensus or an authentic "national interest." On the contrary, a distinguishing feature of most Latin American countries is precisely the absence of any underlying national consensus or any commonly held sense of national identity. Class boundaries continue to cut far more deeply than national boundaries. Empathy and identification with one's fellow citizens often extends no farther than the frontiers of one's own status or occupational group. And political elites, whatever nationalist symbols they may evoke in their public utterance, represent only partial interests and limited class bases. It is a picture, in essence, of subnational communities and ideological divisions that cut through the entire fabric of national societies.

In this fragmented setting, Cuba's relations below the level of formal, intergovernmental diplomacy can fall into a wide variety of possible patterns. The range includes direct dealings, whether open or clandestine, with the Communist parties of the region; alliances with particular subsets of intellectuals and ideologists; and even commercial ties with more pragmatic kinds of entrepreneurial communities. The images that these subcultures hold of Cuba will be equally diverse. For members of ascriptive, traditional elites, the island can only represent a profound symbolic threat to their class-based power and perquisites. For certain clusters of intellectuals, marginalized in repressive political settings, Cuba may be—also at a symbolic level—what Fernando Henrique Cardoso has described as "a hope and an alternative" (1973:2). For other groups of social scientists and analysts, it may come to stand as a concrete alternative to the development models that currently predominate in the Latin American region. As Cuba's relations with Latin America become progressively more open and routinized, the appreciation of Cuba as a meaningful empirical case is likely to gain increasing importance.

Cuban Ideology and National Development

Cuba's developmental trajectory stands in marked contrast to the typical development strategies of most other Latin American countries in the last two decades. The difference cannot be ascribed solely to the fact that Cuba opted for a socialist solution rather than some Latin American variant of the capitalist model. On the contrary, while Cuba's alignment with the Soviet bloc is a fundamentally significant element in the equation, to focus exclusively on the communist-versus-capitalist dimension of the Revolution is to risk missing many of the more unique and subtle shadings in the Cuban experience. The Cuban phenomenon is as much rooted in the island's special historical experiences as in the play of contemporary events, ideologies, and alliances.

In many important respects, prerevolutionary Cuba displayed most of the characteristic features of Latin American underdevelopment. But, in the Cuban case, they were exacerbated by a deep sense of frustrated nationhood and overweening dependence on the island's titanic neighbor. Cuba's deliverance from Spanish colonial rule in 1898 was immediately followed by four years of U.S. military occupation. After a brief period of Cuban self-governance, the U.S. Army returned to administer the island's affairs from 1906 to 1909. Marines were landed in 1912, and again in 1916, to settle internal political conflicts. If the show of force was more restrained in later years, the influence of the United States in Cuban domestic politics nonetheless continued to be inordinate. The notorious Platt Amendment and the Guantánamo naval base were further irritants to Cuban nationalism, persisting reminders that Cuba had yet to achieve full national status and sovereignty over its own destiny. Whether U.S. intentions were generous or imperial, and whether the U.S. presence was benign or baleful, is no longer of much moment; what is important is that U.S. intervention was widely regarded by Cubans as robbing them of their right to self-determination and their national identity. The question of sovereignty would, indeed, later become one of the key threads running through the fabric of *fidelista* ideology.

United States political influence was accompanied by the extraordinary economic dependence of Cuba on the U.S. The sugar quota, if it shielded Cuba from the more severe fluctuations of world market prices, also left Cuba at the mercy of decisions made by the U.S. Congress and the Secretary of Agriculture, who annually determined the fate of the island's sugar crop. Until the Revolution, the United States normally supplied 80 percent of Cuba's imports. In the mid-1950s, U.S. capital controlled 40 percent of Cuba's raw sugar production, 90 percent of telephone, light, and power services, and 50 percent of the public railway system. Cuban subsidiaries of U.S. banks held a quarter of all bank deposits. U.S. corporations played a major role in refining and distribution of petroleum and virtually monopolized the exploitation of Cuba's mineral resources. U.S. capital figured prominently, as well, in manufacturing and merchandising, the production of chemicals, cement, and rubber, cattle ranching, and the lucrative tourist trade (U.S. Department of Commerce 1956).

All Latin American countries in this century have felt the weight of North America's economic presence. In no country was this presence so profound or extensive as in prerevolutionary Cuba. This historical condition, extremely onerous for Cuba's sense of nationhood, does much to explain the approval with which most Cubans greeted the massive expropriation of foreign enterprise that followed on the Revolution. It also helps explain the different meaning with which the Cubans have imbued their current economic dependence on the Soviet Union. As Fidel explained it in a televised interview with Dan Rather, of CBS News, in October 1974:

> How can our relations with the Soviet Union be compared with the relations that existed with the United States? . . .
>
> The United States owned our mines. The United States was the owner of our electric power plants, of our telephone companies, of the main transportation companies, of the principal industries, of the best lands, of the largest sugar mills. They owned our banks, they owned our foreign trade. In a few words, they owned the Cuban economy.
>
> The Soviets do not own a single mine in Cuba, not a single factory, not a single sugar mill, not one hectare of land, not a single bank, not a single business, not a single utility. So, then, all the natural resources,

all the industries, and all the means of production belong to our country and before the revolution they were under the ownership of another country. [*CBS Reports*, "Castro, Cuba and the U.S.A.," 22 October 1974]

It is an explanation that Fidel has publicly offered time and again to the Cuban people, as well as to other members of the Third World who have queried the wisdom of exchanging the economic tutelage of one superpower for that of another. The distinction, in terms of power relationships, is obviously questionable. The Soviet Union, which provides assistance to Cuba at a level of approximately $500 million per year, clearly has immense leverage on the island's economy. In terms of Third World perceptions and the crucial issue of national sovereignty, however, there is indeed a difference. Ownership—whether of mineral resources, airlines, or the Panama Canal—has significant ideological implications in the less developed world. (In the light of recent events, it would seem to have such implications in the developed world as well. An example is the reaction in the United States to Arab proposals for investing their petrodollars in North American enterprises.) Particularly in Latin America, where the United States is seen as a next-door behemoth while the Soviet Union remains a distant, shadowy presence, Fidel's exposition rings truer than most North Americans might suspect.

Cuba's international economic posture and its membership in COMECON are perhaps the most visible manifestations of the island's special trajectory. They add a new wrinkle to geopolitics and they serve to challenge the "geographical fatalism" of other Latin American countries. The more fundamental and distinctive turn of the Cuban phenomenon, however, lies in the internal content of *fidelista* ideology and the direction of national development strategy. The roots of that strategy can be traced back to Fidel Castro's famous speech, "History Will Absolve Me," delivered at the trial following his abortive attack on the Moncada Barracks on 26 July 1953. In that speech, Fidel clearly signalled his commitment to Cuban development; but he did not define it simply as a matter of computable increases in annual GNP. Rather, he saw development as a concept intimately related to such questions as the quality of life and what he called "social justice." Unlike most contemporary technocratic elites, he did not abstract the economy from its sociopolitical context. On the contrary, he explicitly imbued economic matters with political content. Moreover, reversing the orthodox line of reasoning, he treated the deficiencies of the Cuban economy as effect rather than cause. It was not the economy that, by its backwardness, caused social and political distortions in Cuban society; rather, it was the social and political order that kept the economy underdeveloped. Venal public officials, self-serving private businessmen, and a power structure that was repressive, corrupt, and unjust were the obstacles in the way of a prosperous and industrially developed Cuba, capable of satisfying the needs of the entire population—or, as Fidel asserted, of providing "for a population three times as great as it now has" (Castro 1968a:54).

It was a diagnosis that would appall most orthodox economists. Indeed, in later years, Fidel himself would admit his lack of economic expertise and, no doubt with Soviet prodding, would return to the more conventional wisdoms. Before he had done so, however, his earlier order of priorities would have left an indelible stamp on Cuban society. Cuba's social revolution came first; the economic adjustments followed.

The outlines of the social revolution were already visible, albeit diffusely, in the Moncada speech. Addressing his judges, Fidel left no doubt as to the constituency he would choose as his own if he were to achieve power. They were, indeed, explicitly enumerated: the unemployed, the landless rural laborer, the factory worker and the stevedore, the struggling, underpaid teacher, the disaffected intellectual and professional, and the small proprietor. Conspicuously absent from Fidel's list were bankers, businessmen, landlords, and the upper entrepreneurial class in general. He was deliberately aligning himself with the lower strata of Cuban society, with the most disadvantaged and alienated sectors of the population. His constituency, in sum, comprised the great mass of persons who in prerevolutionary Cuba were excluded from the national power structure and only marginally involved, if at all, in the effective national community. As in all less developed countries, they also happened to comprise the majority of the populace.

For anyone who read the speech carefully, it should have been clear that Fidel was not defining a typical, middle-class, reformist movement. If the speech was not pure rhetoric, if he was in fact to make good on his promises to the marginalized sectors of the population, then he would necessarily have to overturn the existing structure of Cuban society. The reallocation of power and participation in a national community is not a kindergarten exercise. Historically, such a transformation has almost always meant revolution.

At the time of the Moncada speech, Fidel's position was more populist than Marxist; it reflected more the influence of José Martí than any Marxian current of thought. As Fidel himself remarked some years later, "It could be called Marxist if you wish, but probably a true Marxist would have said it was not" (Lockwood 1969:159). Idealistic and not especially systematized, *fidelista* ideology in the early stages of the Revolution was not readily classified under one or another formal "ism." Indeed, the *fidelistas* at that time were more often than not in disaccord with the more rigid and orthodox line of the old Communist Party of Cuba. There were, however, certain consistent, discernible strands in their thinking: a commitment to "social justice," a commitment to national sovereignty, and a commitment to extend the frontiers of the national community to include all the hitherto marginal groups in Cuban society. It is questionable whether Fidel, in the first days of the Revolution, clearly foresaw where these concerns would take him. Once operationalized, they would have the effect of alienating the upper classes who had earlier controlled the national power structure and who were less than eager to share their rights and riches with new social groups. As each action produced a counterreaction, the Revolution would become increasingly radicalized. Eventually, the *fidelistas* would be driven into the Soviet camp and to the formal adoption of Marxist-Leninist ideology. In a bipolar world, the options of small, underdeveloped countries are limited. From the vantage of historical hindsight, it now seems unlikely that any other outcome would have been possible for Cuba, once the populist orientation of the Revolution was firmly defined.

In terms of development theory, the significance of these occurrences lies not so much in the realm of geopolitics as in the particular model, or strategy, that emerged in Cuba. In the first years of the Revolution, instead of harnessing the population to the engine of economic growth, the *fidelistas* used the economy as the tool for creating a national political community. Urban reform, agrarian reform, the massive expansion of the educational system, the extension of medical services to the farthest and poorest reaches of the island, and a host of other redistributive measures followed each other with dizzying rapidity. Much of what went on was slapdash and unplanned. Velocity exacted its price in false starts, waste and carelessness, economic inefficiencies, and an overburdening of human competence and capacity. Cuba lost much of its professional manpower, which fled to the United States. The economy became chaotic. Without the massive financial aid of the Soviet Union, it is doubtful that the Cubans would have survived their own experiment.

In retrospect, however, we can now see that if Fidel and his colleagues ran roughshod over their economy in the first years of the Revolution, the net, long-term effect of their policies was to break down the grosser divisions of social class that formerly had fragmented Cuban society and to create an integrated, national citizenry. Even the exodus, so damaging to Cuba in terms of skilled human resources, played its role: the flight of the upper and middle classes automatically opened up social space for those who remained behind, creating a kind of "instant social mobility" in a society that previously had been relatively rigid and closed.

Redistribution and mass participation, rather than economic growth, were the early priorities of the Cuban Revolution. While the exiles fled to the North American mainland, the Cuban leadership instituted a series of radical policies designed to eliminate the social distance and privileges that had hitherto divided the poor from the rich, the illiterate from the educated, the rural from the urban population, and the manual worker from the intellectual. Urban teenagers were sent to the countryside to live with the peasantry during the massive literacy campaign of 1961. University professors and office workers, mobilized for "voluntary labor," paid their dues to the Revolution by cutting cane during the sugar harvest. Peasants were bussed to Havana for special celebrations, and Havana students were sent to secondary schools in the rural provinces. The capital city grew shabby with neglect while major investments were channeled into new construction in the countryside. When the burdens became too great for the economy to bear and severe shortages developed, the *fidelistas* maintained their egalitarian and integrative posture: a rigid system of rationing ensured that scarcity would be equitably shared and that no citizen would lack the basic, minimum requirements for survival. By the mid-1960s, Cubans no longer enjoyed most of the common luxuries of Latin America's upper and middle classes. But Cubans were spared the malnutrition, the short life expectancy, and the grinding ignorance that are the hallmarks of large enclaves of the population elsewhere in the region. If shortages, queues, and a visible lack of creature comforts became the characteristics of the Cuban Revolution, it is nonetheless true that Cuba began to outdistance all other Latin American countries in the spread of primary and secondary education, basic nutrition, and health services.

This egalitarian and distributive trajectory was accompanied by a notable emphasis on popular organization, mobilization, and participation. The Cuban people were expected to behave as citizens, not as marginalized observers of the national process. Few governments in Latin America today would dare to arm the civilian populace; Fidel could do so, creating a citizens' militia, because he had succeeded in creating a genuine national community and a common consciousness of national "interest" and identity. At the Bay of Pigs and in the ensuing periods of isolation, embargo, scarcity, and discomfort, the bulk of the Cuban population responded as a national citizenry. Indeed, one might suggest that these very difficulties and, in particular, the permanent presence of a menacing, hostile power only ninety miles away helped reinforce the shared sense of national purpose and empathy among the island's populace.

The ideological underpinning for this exercise in nation-building was, in December 1961, officially proclaimed to be Marxism-Leninism.

However, at least until 1970, the Cuban reading of Marxist scripture differed considerably from that of their Soviet colleagues. It was more flexible, more voluntaristic, and more radically egalitarian than the ideological position of any orthodox, Soviet-style Communist Party. It was also fiercely independent. As Fidel stated in a speech delivered on 13 March 1967, "this Revolution will never be anybody's satellite or yes-man. It will never ask anybody's permission to maintain its own position, either in matters of ideology, or in domestic or foreign affairs" (Castro 1968b:62). At the time, that assertion was essentially accurate. From all available evidence, it seems certain that the Soviets, throughout the 1960s, were less than happy with the Cuban interpretation of Marxist ideology, their revolutionary tactics in other Latin American countries, and their headstrong, ebullient, egalitarian policies at home. In the Soviet lexicon, the Cuban performance smacked of "petit-bourgeois idealism." Indeed, in 1975, hewing more closely to the Soviet line, Fidel himself would admit that he and his associates had been too "idealistic" in the preceding decade. But, while it lasted, the special, Cuban brand of Marxism served multiple ends inside the Cuban nation-state.

At the most obvious level, Marxism functioned as a central, unifying, national ideology. Modern technocrats may regard ideology as unnecessary baggage in the development process; they do not recognize that their disdain is in fact an ideological statement, an implicit act of faith in technocracy itself. In Cuba, as traditional values were swept away in the maelstrom of revolution, Marxism filled the vacuum. It became a kind of secular religion, knitting the citizenry together in a common belief system. Unlike the theology of "economic growth," which preaches that some citizens should make their fortunes now so that others may get their reward in future generations, Marxism in Cuba served an integrative function, demanding equal sacrifice in the present and promising an equal utopia to the entire populace. At yet another level, Marxism gave "scientific" rationale to the more radical measures of the Cuban leadership, bringing to policy and planning the moral weight of a full-scale philosophical system. Also, by positing an ultimate goal of abundance intertwined with equality, it gave a sense of national purpose to the citizenry, justifying present sacrifices in terms of a future good in which all would share. In an Iberian culture, where work was traditionally considered an unhappy inconvenience, Marxism gave not only respectability, but also positive value to manual and other labor. And, finally, by defining the classless society as the ultimate end of mankind and, more specifically, of Cuban citizens, Marxism gave full license to erase the class divisions that had earlier cut through the fabric of national society.

Thus, what the Cubans did with their egalitarian version of Marxism was first to bring their citizenry into full participation in the national community and to create a national consensus, and only then to devote their total energies to economic development. In so doing, they inverted the conventional line of reasoning that predicates economic advance as the precondition for gradually incorporating marginalized sectors of the population into the national mainstream. The net result, some two decades later, is that Cuba today more closely approximates the standard, textbook definition of a "modern" nation-state than any other Latin American country. Whether one uses aggregate quantitative data, or whether one looks to more subtle, qualitative measures, such as mobilization, participation, integration, and the like, the evidence is there.

The headlong creation of a national community and a national consensus was not, of course, accomplished painlessly. The most obvious price has been the continuing Cuban dependence on Soviet largesse. Geopolitics being what they are, Cuba could not have pursued its special trajectory without Soviet assistance. And the bill for that aid seems to have fallen due. If the Cuban state is now more national and cohesive, it is also clear that in the last several years—or, more precisely, since the gargantuan debacle of the 1970 sugar harvest—the Cubans have adjusted their theory and practice to conform more closely to the Soviet standard. Additionally, to fuse their community together, the Cuban leaders have felt impelled to limit the permissible channels of dissent and to impose an ideological orthodoxy that may well stifle the creativity and innovation that were the initial hallmarks of the Revolution. Political prisoners, a controlled press, and other fetters on free expression must also be put into the balance in weighing the Cuban experience. The Cubans may argue that the relentless pressures of the United States, economic embargo, and hemispheric quarantine forced them to Draconian measures if their revolution was to survive. And they can point to multiple aggregate successes as the trade-off for constraints on individuals. It should be recognized, moreover, that the strictures the Cubans may place on the free and full exercise of individual civil liberties will not have the same resonance in contemporary Latin America as they perhaps might have in North America and most of Western Europe. In a region where dictatorial government, censorship, arbitrary imprisonment, and even torture have become increasingly commonplace in the last decade, the Cuban regime will seem benign by comparison. For many Latin Americans, the price the Cubans have paid for national cohesion and their own variety of "development" will not appear unduly exorbitant.

Some Implications for Future Hemispheric Relations

The consolidation of the Cuban Revolution and the institutionalization of social and political processes will necessarily affect Cuba's external comportment in the Americas. Certain indicative signals are already clear in the pronouncements of the Cuban leadership and in Cuba's general diplomatic behavior in the hemisphere. Accordingly, while one should not underestimate the capacity of the Cubans to surprise observers by executing startling turnabouts on specific issues, one can nonetheless discern consistent patterns in their overall posture and thus hazard a number of educated guesses about the factors that will most strongly influence the direction of foreign policy in the Americas over the coming few years.

First, we can presume that the internal maturation of the Cuban system, the emergence of fixed governmental processes and structures, and the routinization of bureaucratic procedure will be reflected in Cuba's external conduct. In the international arena, the island is already behaving less like a maverick and more like a mature nation-state. Cuban diplomats no longer cavort in battle fatigues, nor do they pluck chickens in hotel corridors. Audacious, impromptu adventures in the Bolivian highlands or in the surrounding Caribbean islands have given way to more structured relations with governments and increasing recourse to normal diplomatic channels and procedures. Cuban policy in the Americas is likely to be more coherent and predictable in the future, the product of a stable domestic system and a well-defined "national interest." This diagnosis should not be taken to mean that the Cubans will henceforth refrain from clandestine activities and more overt kinds of mischief on the foreign front. (Cuba's African entanglements are empirical evidence to the contrary.) But such antics are less likely in the future to be ad hoc, personalistic, or out of phase with other foreign-policy initiatives. For better or for worse, we can expect that the *process* by which foreign activities are determined will be more consistent and impersonal. And revolutionary romanticism will increasingly give way to more conventional logic in the conduct of international affairs. Cuba's involvements in Africa do not contradict this thesis; whether one deplores or applauds the Cuban presence in Angola or Ethiopia, it certainly is neither an impromptu nor a romantic adventure by a ragged collection of visionaries. Rather, it is a carefully calculated and orchestrated exercise in foreign policy, realistically reflecting the balance among opportunity, probable risk, and potential benefit. One can presume that a similar realism will govern Cuban initiatives in the Western Hemisphere.

Second, all available evidence suggests that Cuba is less likely now than in the past to pursue a foreign trajectory that deviates in any substantial degree from the policy stance of the Soviet Union. Domestically, the influence of Soviet theory and practice is evident in the muting of the rampant egalitarianism that earlier characterized Cuban Marxism. Material incentives have come back into play. Production norms and price policy are now attuned more closely to standard Soviet practice. One can logically expect that the influence visible in domestic affairs will carry over into the international arena. Certainly, the Cuban incursion in Africa is consistent with Soviet interests in that continent. The implications for Cuban policy in the Americas are similar and several, reflecting the lack of Soviet enthusiasm for any serious military embroilment or confrontation in the region. Among other things, the Cubans will probably maintain a more congenial posture toward those governments of Latin America that are not fanatically repressive and anti-Marxist. It also is likely that the Cubans will have closer ties than before with the orthodox Communist parties of the region, rather than with ultra-left revolutionary movements. Significantly, Latin America's Soviet-linked Communist parties have traditionally been more willing than many independent, radical leftist groups to make alliances with bourgeois governments and parties. Indeed, their tractability on this score was once a source of bitter criticism by the *fidelistas*. It no longer is.

Third, as both external and internal threats diminish, the Cubans can afford to be more self-confident and flexible in their international posture. In the mid-1960s, with the Revolution embattled and facing difficulties on a wide variety of fronts, Cuba's attempts to foment revolutionary movements elsewhere in the hemisphere were justified not only by ideology, but also by a natural, tactical need to divert the forces and attention of the "enemy." With its greater economic and strategic security, Cuba today can be more relaxed and patient. If socialism throughout the Americas is still the ultimate goal, it can be deferred for a time without necessarily prejudicing Cuba's defenses and situation.

Fourth, as the Cubans have demonstrated over the last two decades, they are pragmatic and ultimately rational in their comportment. There are certain basic ideological issues on which they will not give way—most notably their own national sovereignty and their rejection of capitalism within their own borders. But they have proven themselves time and again to be capable of shifting tactical gears in the face of objective circumstances. Cuba's domestic past is littered with the debris of policies that were tested, found wanting, and discarded. One can reasonably expect them to be similarly practical in their international posture. The unhappy conclusion of Che Guevara's attempt to launch a guerrilla front in Bolivia and the equally unhappy conclusion of the Allende experiment in Chile are lessons that are not likely to be lost on the Cubans.

Against this backdrop, it now seems possible to predict that Cuba's policies in the hemisphere will be more flexible in the future and more realistically attuned to the subtle differences and prospects encountered among the Latin American republics. As early as 1973, Fidel Castro signalled the probable new direction of Cuba's activities in the Americas: cordial relations with those countries willing to accept Cuba on its own terms; and a supportive posture toward any government willing to demonstrate its independence of the United States. Addressing a mass rally in Havana on 1 May 1973, Fidel said:

> Can [there] be forms of cooperation between Cuba and other Latin American countries, even though those countries have not yet arrived at socialism? We believe so, we believe that many forms of cooperation can be developed between the Cuban Revolution and other Latin American governments, providing those governments adopt an attitude of independence, a sovereign attitude, an attitude in defense of their national interests against the United States. [Castro 1973:8]

That statement continues to characterize Cuba's posture in the hemisphere, and it is likely to remain operative for some time to come. The other side of the coin, of course, is that, in the intervening period, many Latin American governments have come to accept Cuba's new stance and to welcome the island back as a functioning member of the inter-American system. It is an explicit recognition of Cuba's maturity and stability, and an implicit indication of the changing climate in the Americas since the United States in 1962 could mobilize sufficient votes to expel Cuba from the OAS.

By way of final soothsaying, we can probably predict the eventual resumption of relations between Cuba and the United States. But they will no doubt be characterized by a substantial element of ambivalence. Tactical accommodations can probably be reached on the host of issues now pending between the two countries. But it is unlikely that Cuba will forget the accumulated store of historical grievances that extend back to the last century. Nor are the Cubans likely to give up their vision of *nuestra América* as a Latin counterweight to the northern colossus.

References

Cardoso, Fernando Henrique. 1973. "Cuba: Lesson or Symbol?" (Module 267.) In David P. Barkin and Nita R. Manitzas, eds., *Cuba: The Logic of the Revolution*. Andover, Mass.: Warner Modular Publications.
Castro, Fidel. 1968a. *History Will Absolve Me*. London: Jonathan Cape.

———. 1968b. *Those Who Are Not Revolutionary Fighters Cannot Be Called Communists*. New York: Merit Publishers.

———. 1973. Speech in Havana, 1 May 1973. Reprinted in *Cuba Resource Center Newsletter* 3, no. 4 (November).

Lockwood, Lee. 1969. *Castro's Cuba, Cuba's Fidel*. New York: Vintage Books.

Silvert, Kalman H. 1975. "The Relevance of Latin American Domestic Politics to North American Foreign Policy." In *The Americas in a Changing World*. New York: Quadrangle. Reprinted in *Essays in Understanding Latin America*. Philadelphia: Institute for the Study of Human Issues, 1977.

U.S. Department of Commerce. 1956. *Investment in Cuba*. Washington, D.C.: Government Printing Office.

Index